BURT FRANKLIN: RESEARCH & SOURCE WORKS SERIES
American Classics in History and Social Science 253

NORTH AMERICAN
INDIANS OF THE PLAINS

ASSINIBOIN WARRIOR
(After Maximilian.)

NORTH AMERICAN INDIANS OF THE PLAINS

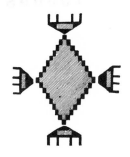

By CLARK WISSLER

CURATOR OF ANTHROPOLOGY

BURT FRANKLIN REPRINTS

New York, N. Y.

ANTHROPOLOGICAL HANDBOOK FUND

HANDBOOK SERIES No. 1
(THIRD EDITION, SECOND PRINTING)

Published by LENOX HILL Pub. & Dist. Co. (Burt Franklin)
235 East 44th St., New York, N.Y. 10017
Reprinted: 1974
Printed in the U.S.A.

Burt Franklin: Research and Source Works Series
American Classics in History and Social Science 253

Library of Congress Cataloging in Publication Data

Wissler, Clark, 1870-1947.
    North American Indians of the Plains.

    Reprint of the 1934 ed. published by American Museum of Natural
History, New York, which was issued as no. 1 of its Handbook series.
    Bibliography: p.
    1. Indians of North America—Great Plains. I. Title. II. Series: American
Museum of Natural History, New York. Handbook series, no. 1.
E78.G73W57 1974   970.4'78   73-22043
ISBN 0-8337-5361-4

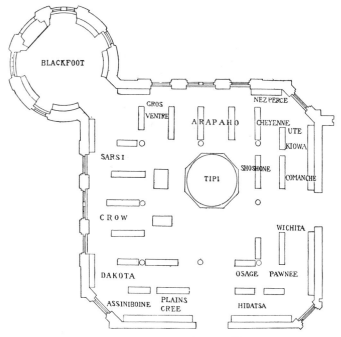

PLAN OF THE PLAINS INDIAN HALL.

The Museum exhibits for the various tribes are arranged in approximate geographical order, beginning with the Plains-Cree of the north and proceeding with the typical nomadic tribes (p. 13). In the northwestern part of the hall are the Shoshoni, Ute, and Nez Percé, whose culture is intermediate between that of the Plains and Plateau area. In the northeastern section are the Mandan, Hidatsa, and other Village tribes, also manifesting an intermediate culture between the Plains and that of the Woodlands to the east.

The Woodland hall to the east and the Southwest hall to the north are so arranged as to bring the intermediate tribes of each region near the entrance to the Plains Indian hall. Thus, from case to case, one may follow changes in culture from the Atlantic Coast to the Colorado River and the Gulf of California.

3

PREFACE.

THIS little book is not merely a guide to museum collections from the Plains Indians, but a summary of the facts and interpretations making up the anthropology of those Indians. The specimens in this Museum were, for the most part, systematically collected by members of the scientific staff while sojourning among the several tribes. They were selected to illustrate various points in tribal life and customs, or culture. The exhibits in the Plains Hall contain, as far as space permits, most of the typical objects for each tribe; yet it has been physically impossible to show everything the Museum possesses. So the most characteristic objects for each tribe have been selected and care taken to have the other objects common to many tribes appear at least once in some part of the hall. The ideal way would be to get every variety of every object used by each subdivision of a tribe and exhibit all of them in their entirety; but few collections can be made so complete, and even if they could, space in the building could not be found for them. The exhibits, then, should be taken as material indices, or marks, of tribal cultures and not as complete expositions of them. This handbook, on the other hand, deals with the main points in the anthropology of the Plains Indians many of which (as marriage, social and political organization, language, etc.) cannot be demonstrated by collections. The statements in the text are made upon the authority of the many special students of these Indians in whose writings will be found far more complete accounts. Citations to the more important works will be given in the bibliography. The illustrations are chiefly from the anthropological publications of the Museum and for the most part represent specimens on exhibition in the Plains Hall. For a mere general view of the subject, the legends to the maps, the introduction, and the concluding chapter are recommended. The intervening topics may then be taken up as guides to the study of collections or the perusal of the special literature.

CONTENTS.

CHAPTER I.

CHAPTER II.

CHAPTER III.

CHAPTER IV.

CHAPTER V.

CHAPTER VI.

CHAPTER VII.

CHAPTER VIII.

MAPS AND ILLUSTRATIONS.

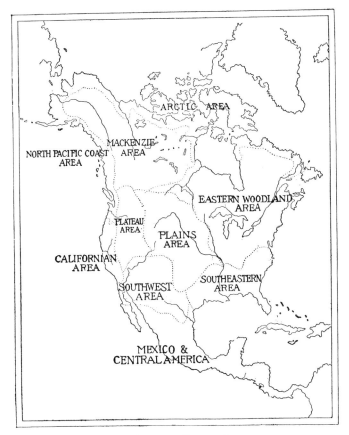

CULTURE AREAS IN NORTH AMERICA.

The divisions marked on this map are not absolute but relative. Rarely can a tribe be found anywhere that does not share some of the cultural traits of all its immediate neighbors. Yet, certain groups of tribes often have highly characteristic traits in common; hence, they are said to be of the same general culture type. Thus the tribes discussed in this book have a number of peculiar traits whose distribution in more or less complete association is taken as indicating the geographical extent of a type of culture. The fact that these boundaries almost coincide with the limits of the treeless prairies and plains

11

and that this culture is most intensified among the tribes living in the Great Plains, has given rise to the term Plains area. In the same way other parts of the continent appear as the homes of peculiar culture types. Anthropologists generally recognize at least eleven such areas whose approximate extents we have indicated in the accompanying map. The types for each of these are illustrated as space permits in the four halls on the first floor of the Museum. As will be exemplified in the text, the lines separating these areas are somewhat arbitrary. A more correct method would be to color the areas and divide them by broad bands in ever changing mixtures of the two colors, but only in a few instances have we sufficient data to do even this accurately. Hence, the approximate line seems the best designation of culture boundaries.

Reference to a linguistic map of North America will show that there is little correspondence between linguistic stocks and culture type, for while in some cases the two lines on the map coincide, in others, they show no approach whatsoever. Again, while the physical types of the Indians show some tendencies to agree in distribution with cultural traits, they also show marked disagreements. Hence, it is not far wrong to say that if, according to the data now available, we superimposed cultural, linguistical, and physical type maps, we should find them with few boundaries in common.

Returning to the consideration of culture areas and referring to the tribal map (p. 13), we see that the tribes of Plains Indians in a central position are the most typical, while their immediate neighbors show tendencies to live like more distant tribes. What we find, then, is a kind of culture center, where the purest types are found, while surrounding this center are less pure cultures. Each of the designated culture areas in North America contains such a center where the true type of culture is to be found.

A visitor to the Museum, walking through the exhibition halls for the American Indians, will note contrasts in the objects shown as he passes from one to the other. Taking the Plains Indian Hall as the point of departure, he will note that as he approaches the Woodland Hall to the east, there is a change in the contents of the cases, and when well within the latter, the resemblances to the Plains Indian Hall cease. The same is true, if one turns northward in the Plains Hall and passes into the Southwest Area, where the Apache remind one of the Plains, but as one passes on to the cases for the Pueblo tribes, the resemblances soon fade out altogether. In this way one may come into an understanding of what is meant by the term, culture area.

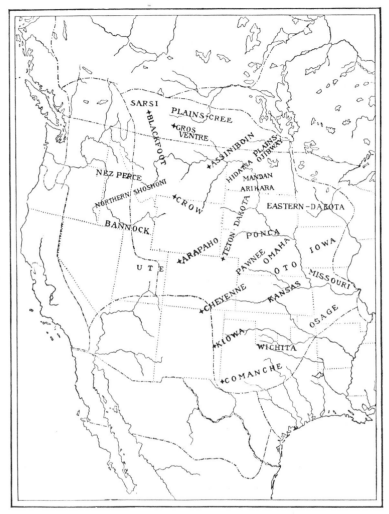

THE INDIANS OF THE PLAINS.

The ranges for the various tribes are approximately indicated by the positions and extents of their respective names. As a rule, these tribes did not respect definite boundaries to their ranges, each tribe claiming certain camping places, but otherwise hunting and roaming where it pleased. The typical Plains tribes are designated by a star and range north and south across the area. To the east of them are the tribes practising some agriculture, perhaps in imitation of the Woodland tribes. On the west are a few tribes whose position is uncertain; hence, the boundary for the culture area has been drawn through their range, thus giving them an intermediate position.

13

THE DISTRIBUTION OF FORESTS IN WESTERN UNITED STATES.

The shaded portions of this map mark the areas originally covered with trees. The true plains extend from north to south along the eastern border of the Rocky Mountains. On the west, trees are found on the sides of mountains; on the east, they stretch out into the plains along the margins of the streams. Reference to the tribal map shows how the typical group ranges in the open plains while the eastern agricultural Village group lives in the partially forested belt. On the west the Plateau group appears to range in the open stretches among the mountains.

14

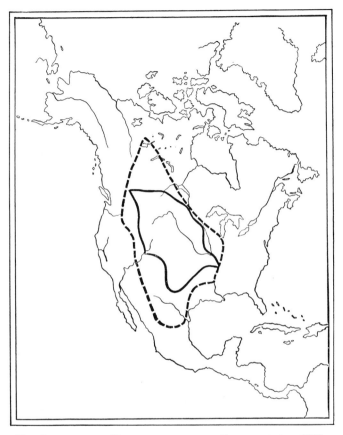

MAP SHOWING THE DISTRIBUTION OF THE BUFFALO ABOUT 1800.

The larger area defines the limits of the buffalo range in 1800 as determined by Dr. J. A. Allen. The smaller area indicates the range of the Plains Indians. While the bison area is somewhat larger than the culture area, the largest herds were found within the bounds of the latter. On the other hand, the cultures of tribes along the borders of the area are often intermediate in character. Hence, we find a rather close correlation between the distribution of the bison and culture traits, the nine typical tribes living where the herds were thickest.

15

INTRODUCTION.

THE North American Indians may be classified in three ways: first, as to language; second, as to customs and habits (culture); third, as to anatomical characters (physical type). It is, however, usual to consider them as composed of small more or less distinct political or social groups, or tribes, and it is under such group names that the objects in museum collections are arranged. The cultures of many tribes are quite similar and since such resemblances are nearly always found among neighbors and not among widely scattered tribes, it is convenient and proper to group them in geographical or culture areas. Most anthropologists classify the cultures of North American tribes approximately as shown on the accompanying map.

In the region of the great plains and prairies were many tribes of Plains Indians, who have held the first place in the literature and art of our time. Being rather war-like and strong in numbers, many of them are intimately associated with the history of our western states and every school boy knows how the Dakota (Sioux) rode down Custer's command. The names of Sitting-bull, Red-cloud, and Chief Joseph are also quite familiar.

The culture of these Plains tribes is most strikingly associated with the buffalo, or bison, which not so very long ago roamed over their entire area. Turning to the map one may see how closely the distributions of this culture type and that for the buffalo coincide. This animal supplied them with one of their chief foods, in accessible and almost never-failing abundance. For a part of the year at least, all Plains tribes used the conical skin tent, or tipi. In early times the dog was used to transport baggage and supplies, but later, horses became very abundant and it is not far wrong to speak of all Plains tribes as horsemen. When on the hunt or moving in a large body most of these tribes were controlled by a band of "soldiers," or police, who drove in stragglers and repressed those too eager to advance and who also policed the camp and maintained order and system in the tribal hunt. All Indians are quite religious. Most of the Plains tribes had a grand annual gathering known in literature as the sun dance. In general, these few main cultural characteristics may be taken to designate the type— the use of the buffalo, the tipi, the horse, the soldier-band, and the sun dance. Many of the tribes living near the Mississippi and along the Missouri practised agriculture in a small way and during a part of the year lived in earth-covered or bark houses. Furthermore, there are many other tribal differences, so that it becomes admissible to subdivide the Plains Indians. The following seems the most consistent grouping.

1. The Northern Tribes

*Assiniboin	Plains-Cree
*Blackfoot	Plains-Ojibway
*Crow	Sarsi
*Gros Ventre	*Teton-Dakota

2. The Southern Tribes

*Arapaho	*Comanche
*Cheyenne	*Kiowa
	Kiowa-Apache

3. The Village, or Eastern Tribes

Arikara	Omaha
Hidatsa	Osage
Iowa	Oto
Kansa	Pawnee
Mandan	Ponca
Missouri	Eastern Dakota
	Wichita

4. The Plateau, or Western Tribes

Bannock	Northern Shoshoni
Nez Percé	Ute
	Wind River Shoshoni

Cultural characteristics change gradually as we go from one tribe to another; hence, on the edges of the Plains area we may expect many doubtful cases. Among such may be enumerated the Flathead and

Pend D'Oreille of the northwest, the Illinois and Winnebago of the east, and some Apache of the south. On the southeast, in Texas and Arkansas, were the Caddoan tribes (Kichai, Waco, Tawakoni, etc., relatives of the Wichita) having a culture believed to be intermediate between the Plains and that of the Southeastern area. Yet, in spite of these and other doubtful cases, it is usual to exclude all not enumerated in the above lists as belonging more distinctly with other culture areas. As this grouping is rather for convenience than otherwise, and the culture of each tribe is determined by its own data, the exact placing of these border tribes is of no great moment. However, the most typical Plains tribes are the Assiniboin, Blackfoot, Gros Ventre, Crow, Teton-Dakota, Arapaho, Cheyenne, Comanche, and Kiowa, indicated in the preceding list by an asterisk (*). Reference to the map shows how peculiarly this typical group stretches from north to south, almost in a straight line, with the intermediate Plateau group on one side and the Village group on the other. Again, the forestry map shows that the range of this typical nomadic group coincides with the area in which trees are least in evidence. It embraces the true tipi-dwelling, horse, and non-agricultural tribes. It is primarily the cultural traits of this nomadic group that are discussed in this book, though the important exceptions among the two marginal groups are noted.

CHAPTER I.

MATERIAL CULTURE.

SINCE this is a discussion of the general characteristics of Plains Indians, we shall not take them up by tribes, as is usual, but by topics. Anthropologists are accustomed to group the facts of primitive life under the following main heads: material culture (food, transportation, shelter, dress, manufactures, weapons, etc.), social organization, religion and ceremonies, art, language, and physical type.

Food. The flesh of the buffalo was the great staple of the Plains Indians, though elk, antelope, bear and smaller game were not infrequently used. On the other hand, vegetable foods were always a considerable portion of their diet, many of the eastern groups cultivating corn (maize) and gathering wild rice, the others making extensive use of wild roots, seeds, and fruits. All the tribes living on the edges of the buffalo area, even those on the western border of the Woodlands, seem to have made regular hunting excursions out into the open country. Thus Nicolas Perrot writing in 1680–1718 (p. 119) says of the Indians in Illinois:—

The savages set out in the autumn, after they have gathered the harvest, to go hunting; and they do not return to their villages until the month of March, in order to plant the grain on their lands. As soon as this is done, they go hunting again, and do not return until the month of July.

21

Early explorers in the plateaus to the west of the plains tell us that the Nez Percé and Flathead of Idaho and even the inhabitants of the Rio Grande pueblo of Taos, New Mexico, made periodical hunting excursions to the plains.

To most of the Plains tribes, the introduction of the European horse was a great boon. Unfortunately, we have no definite information as to when and how the horse was spread over the plains but it was so early that its presence is noted by some of the earliest explorers. It is generally assumed that by trade and by the capture of horses escaping from the settlements, the various tribes quickly acquired their stock, first from Mexico and the southern United States, whence the Apache, Comanche, Kiowa, and Pawnee obtained them, and in turn passed them on to the north. The Shoshoni and other tribes of the Plateau area were also pioneers in their use. Even as early as 1754 horses are reported in great numbers among the Blackfoot, one of the extreme Northern Plains groups. Hence, we have no detailed information as to the mode of life among these tribes before the horse was introduced, except what is gleaned from their tribal traditions. That the use of the horse made a great change in culture is quite probable. It must have stimulated roving and the pursuit of the buffalo and discouraged tendencies toward fixed abodes and agriculture.

Buffalo Hunting. All Plains tribes seem to have practised coöperative hunting in an organized military-like manner. This usually took the form of a surround in which a large body of Indians on swift horses and under the direction of skilled leaders rode round and round a herd bunching them up and shooting down the animals one by one. Stirring accounts of such hunts have been left us by such eye-witnesses as Catlin, James, and Grinnell. All tribes seem to have used this method in summer and it was almost the only one followed by the Southern Plains tribes.

In winter, however, when the northern half of the plains was often covered with snow, this method was not practised. Alexander Henry, Maximilian, and others, have described a favorite winter method of impounding, or driving the herd into an enclosure. Early accounts indicate that the Plains-Cree and Assiniboin were the most adept in driving into these enclosures and may perhaps have introduced the method among the Plains tribes. The Plains-Cree are but a small outlying part of a very widely distributed group of Cree, the culture of whose main body seems quite uniform. Now, even the Cree east of Hudson Bay, Canada, use a similar method for deer, and since there is every reason to believe that the Plains-Cree are but a colony of the larger body to the east, it seems fair to assume that the method of impounding buffalo originated with them. However that may be, some form of it was practised by the Blackfoot, Gros Ventre, Hidatsa, Mandan, Teton-Dakota, Arapaho, Cheyenne, and perhaps others.

We have some early accounts of another method used in the prairies of Illinois and Iowa. Thus, in Perrot (121) we read:—

When the village has a large number of young men able to bear arms they divide these into three bodies; one takes its route to the right, another that to the left, and half of the third party is divided between the two former ones. One of these latter parties goes away [from its main column] a league or thereabout to the right, and the other remains on the left, both parties forming, each on its own side, a long file; then they set out, in single file, and continue their march until they judge that their line of men is sufficiently long for them to advance into the depths [of the forest]. As they begin their march at midnight, one of the parties waits until dawn, while the others pursue their way; and after they have marched a league or more another party waits again for daylight; the rest march [until] after another half-league has been covered, and likewise wait. When the day has at last begun, this third party which had separated to the right and the left with the two others pushes its way farther; and as soon as the rising sun has dried off the dew on the ground, the parties on the right and the left, being in sight of each other, come together in [one] file, and close up the end of the circuit which they intend to surround.

They commence at once by setting fire to the dried herbage which is abundant in those prairies; those who occupy the flanks do the same; and at that moment the entire village breaks camp, with all the old men and young boys—who divide themselves equally on both sides, move away to a distance, and keep the hunting parties in sight so that they can act with the latter, so that the fires can be lighted on all four sides at once and gradually communicate the flames one to another. That produces the same effect to the sight as four ranks of palisades, in which the buffaloes are enclosed. When the savages see that the animals are trying to get outside of it, in order to escape the fires which surround them on all sides (and this is the one thing in the world which they most fear), they run at them and compel them to reënter the enclosure; and they avail themselves of this method to kill all the beasts. It is asserted that there are some villages which have secured as many as fifteen hundred buffaloes, and others more or fewer, according to the number of men in each and the size of the enclosure which they make in their hunting.

The natural inference seems to be that the grass firing and impounding methods of taking buffalo were developed before the introduction of the horse and are therefore the most primitive. The individual hunting of buffalo as well as in small parties was, of course, practised. In modern times swift horses were used to bring the rider in range when he shot down the fleeing beasts. But before horses were known the coöperative method must have prevailed.

Hunting Implements. The implements used for killing buffalo were not readily displaced by guns. Bows and arrows were used long after guns were common. In fact, pioneers maintain that at close range the rapidity and precision of the bow was only to be excelled by the repeating rifle, a weapon developed in the 70's. Even so, the bow was not entirely discarded until the buffalo became extinct. The bows were of two general types: the plain wooden bow, and the sinew-backed, or compound bow. It is generally held that the tribes east of the Mississippi River used the simple wooden bow while those on the Pacific Coast used the sinew-backed type. It is quite natural, therefore, that among the Plains tribes we should find both types in general use and that the sinew-backed was more common among the Shoshoni and other Plateau tribes.

Some curious bows were made from mountain sheep horn backed with sinew, a fine example of which is to be seen in the Nez Percé collection (Fig. 1). The Crow, Hidatsa, and Mandan sometimes used a bow of elkhorn, probably one of the finest examples of Indian workmanship: "They take a large horn or prong, and saw a slice off each side of it; these slices are then filed or rubbed down until the flat sides fit nicely together, when they are glued

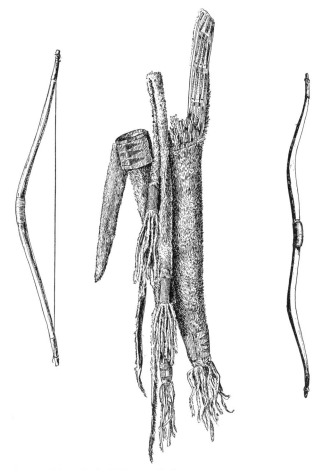

Fig. 1. Sinew-backed Bow and Quiver from the Blackfoot and a Compound Bow of Mountain Sheep Horn from the Nez Percé.

and wrapped at the ends. Four slices make a bow, it being jointed. Another piece of horn is laid on the center of the bow at the grasp, where it is glued fast. The whole is then filed down until it is perfectly proportioned, when the white bone is ornamented, carved, and painted. Nothing can exceed the beauty of these bows, and it takes an Indian

Fig. 2. Lance with Obsidian Point. Nez Percé.

about three months to make one." (Belden, 112.) All these compound bows are sinew-backed, it being the sinew that gives them efficiency. Some fine old wooden bows may be seen in the Museum's Dakota collection.

A lance was frequently used for buffalo: in the hands of a powerful horseman, this is said to have been quite effective. There is a stone-pointed lance in the Nez Percé collection which may be of the type formerly used, Fig. 2. Wounded animals and those in the enclosure of the pound were often brought down by knocking on the head with stone-headed clubs and mauls.

Pemmican. As buffalo could not be killed every day, some method of preserving their flesh in an eatable condition was necessary to the well-being of the Plains Indian. The usual method was by drying in the sun. Steaks were cut broad and thin, and slashed by short cuts which gaped open when the pieces were suspended, giving the appearance of holes. These steaks were often placed in boiling water for a few moments and then hung upon poles

Fig. 3.   Meat Drying Rack.   Blackfoot.

or racks out of reach of dogs. In the course of a few days, if kept free from moisture, the meat became hard and dry. It could then be stored in bags for future use. Fat, also, could be dried if slightly boiled.

Dried meat of the buffalo and sometimes of the elk was often pounded fine, making what was known as pemmican. While some form of pemmican was used in many parts of North America, the most charac-

teristic kind among the Plains Indians was the berry
pemmican.   To make this, the best cuts of the buffalo were dried in the usual manner.   During the
berry season wild cherries (*Prunus demissa*) were
gathered and crushed with stones, pulverizing the

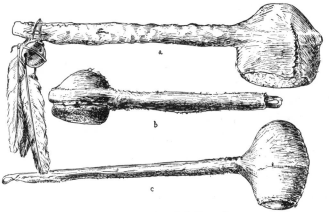

Fig. 4.   Stone-headed Pounders.

pits, and reducing the whole to a thick paste which
was partially dried in the sun.   Then the dried meat
was softened by holding over a fire, after which it
was pounded fine with a stone or stone-headed maul.
In the Dakota collection may be seen some interesting rawhide mortars for this purpose.   This pulver-
ized meat was mixed with melted fat and marrow, to
which was added the dried but sticky cherry paste.
The whole mass was then packed in a long, flat rawhide bag, called a parfleche.   With proper care, such
pemmican would keep for years.   In pioneer days,
it was greatly prized by white trappers and soldiers.

Agriculture. Almost without exception, the Village group of tribes made at least some attempts to cultivate maize. Of the northern tribes, none have been credited with this practice, except perhaps the Teton-Dakota. Yet, the earlier observers usually distinguish the Teton from the Eastern Dakota by their non-agricultural habits. Of the southern tribes, we cannot be so sure. The Cheyenne, who seem to have abandoned a forest home for the plains just before the historic period, have traditions of maize culture, but seem to have discontinued it soon after going into the buffalo country. The Arapaho are thought by some anthropologists to have preceded the Cheyenne. Yet while many writers are disposed to admit that all of the southern group may have made some attempts at maize growing, they insist that these were feeble in comparison with the Village tribes. When, however, we turn to the Plateau area, there are no traces of maize growing. In association with maize it was usual to raise some varieties of squash and beans.

Thus, in a general way, the practice of agriculture seems to dwindle out gradually as we leave the more fertile river bottoms of the east and south, suggesting that its positive absence among the extreme western and northern tribes is due to unfavorable soil and climate rather than to any mental or social differences in the tribes concerned. This is consistent with the wide distribution of tobacco raising. The Blackfoot, Crow, Hidatsa, Mandan, Arikara,

Pawnee, and Eastern Dakota are known to have cultivated it for ceremonial purposes.

The plants have not been closely studied, but that of the Hidatsa and Mandan is *Nicotiana quadrivalvis*. It is probable that this is the species among the other tribes, with the exception of the Crow and Blackfoot. The latter has been pronounced *Nicotiana attenuata* and Crow tobacco is *multivalvis*. The last is said to be a native of Oregon and to have been cultivated by tribes in the Columbia River valley. The fact that the Blackfoot and Crow did not attempt any other agriculture except the raising of this tobacco rather strengthens the previous opinion that maize was not produced because of the unfavorable conditions. Among the tribes of the Plateau area, on the western border of the Plains, wild seeds and grains were gathered and so took the place of maize in the east. So we find the Shoshoni and Ute making some use of such foods. On the other hand, the northern and southern Plains groups depended mostly upon dried berries and edible roots, which, however, were a relatively small part of their diet, buffalo flesh being the important food. This was particularly true of the nine typical tribes. With these tribes, the buffalo was not only food, but his by-products, such as skin, bones, hair, horns, and sinew, were the chief materials for costume, tents, and utensils of all kinds.

Transportation. Before the introduction of the horse, the Plains Indians traveled on foot. The

tribes living along the Mississippi made some use of
canoes, according to early accounts, while those of
the Missouri and inland used only crude tub-like

Fig. 5.   Crossing the Missouri in a Bull-Boat.
(Wilson photo.)

affairs for ferry purpose. When first discovered,
the Mandan, Hidatsa, and Arikara had villages on
the Missouri, in what is now North Dakota, but they
have never been credited with canoes. For crossing the river, they used the bull-boat, a tub-shaped

affair made by stretching buffalo skins over a
wooden frame; but journeys up and down the bank
were made on foot. Many of the Eastern Dakota
used small canoes in gathering wild rice in the small
lakes of Minnesota, though the Teton-Dakota have
not been credited with the practice. It seems probable that the ease of travel in the open plains and
the fact that the buffalo were often to be found inland, made the use of canoes impractical, whereas
along the great lakes the broad expanse of water
offered every advantage to their use. Since almost
every Plains tribe used some form of the bull-boat
for ferrying, and many of them came in contact with
canoe-using Indians, the failure of those living along
the Missouri to develop the canoe can scarcely be
attributed to ignorance.

When on the march, baggage was carried on the
human back and also by dogs, the only aboriginal
domestic animals. Most tribes used a peculiar A-
shaped contrivance, known as a dog travois, upon
which packs were placed. All the northern tribes
are credited with the dog travois. Many of the Village tribes also used it, as did also some of the southern group. With the introduction of the horse, a
larger but similar travois was used. This, however,
did not entirely displace the dog travois as Catlin's
sketches show Indians on the march with both horses
and dogs harnessed to travois. The travois of the
northern tribes were of two types: rectangular
cross-frames and oval netted frames, Fig. 6. The

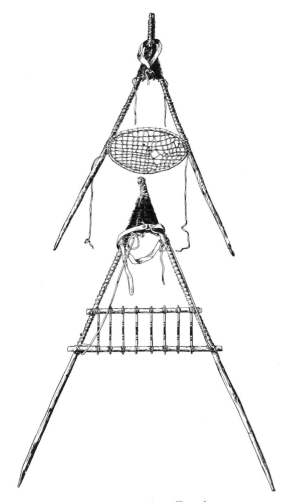

Fig. 6. Blackfoot Travois.

Blackfoot, Sarsi and Gros Ventre inclined toward the former; the Assiniboin, Dakota, Hidatsa, and Mandan toward the latter, though both types were often used simultaneously. On the other hand, the southern tribes seem to have inclined toward an improvised travois formed by binding tipi poles to the

Fig. 7.   Assiniboin Dog Travois.

sides of the saddle and slinging the pack across behind.

The use of a sled on the ice or snow has not been credited to any except some of the Eastern Dakota and the Mandan and among them it is quite probable that it was introduced by white traders.

The riding gear and horse trappings that always form an interesting part of collections naturally

came in with the horse and followed European
models. The native bridle was a simple rope or
thong looped around the jaw. Saddles were of two
types: pads and frames. The latter were made of
wood or elkhorn securely bound with fresh buffalo
hide which shrunk as it dried. The Mills Catlin collection contains a sketch showing how one of the
saddles is staked down to the ground while the wet
rawhide sets in place. Women's saddles had very
high pommels and were often gaily ornamented.
Stirrups were also made of wood bound with rawhide. Some tribes, the Dakota for example, used
highly decorated saddle blankets, or skins; while
others (Crow, Blackfoot, etc.) used elaborate crup-
pers. Quirts with short handles of elkhorn or wood
were common. In fact, there was little difference
in the form of riding gear among all the Plains
tribes.

The nine typical tribes were more or less always
on the move. All their possessions were especially
designed for ready transport. Nearly all recepta-
cles and most utensils were made of rawhide, while
the tipi, or tent, was easily rolled up and placed
upon a travois. When the chief gave out the order
to break camp it took but a few minutes for the
women to have everything loaded on travois and
ready for the march. Even the Village group used
tipis and horses when on the buffalo hunt (p. 19).
The smaller baggage was often loaded upon dog
travois. We have no accurate data as to how the

camp was moved before horses came into the country, but the process was certainly more laborious and the marches shorter.

The Tipi. One of the most characteristic features of Plains Indian culture was the tipi. All the tribes of the area, almost without exception, used it for a part of the year at least. Primarily, the tipi was a conical tent covered with dressed buffalo skins. A carefully mounted and equipped tipi from the Blackfoot Indians stands in the center of the Plains exhibit. Everywhere the tipi was made, cared for, and set up by the women. First, a conical framework of long slender poles was erected and the cover raised into place. Then the edges of the cover were staked down and the poles supporting the "ears" put in place. The "ears" are wings, or flies, to keep the wind out of the smoke hole at the top; they were moved about by the outside poles. The fire was built near the center and the beds spread upon the ground around the sides. The head of the family usually sat near the rear, or facing the door.

While in essential features the tipis of all Plains tribes were the same, there were nevertheless some important differences. Thus, when setting up a tipi, the Beaver, Blackfoot, Blood, Comanche, Crow, Hidatsa, Omaha, Piegan, Sarsi, Shoshoni, and Ute first tie four poles as a support to the others; while the Arapaho, Arikara, Assiniboin, Cheyenne, Gros Ventre, Kiowa, Mandan, Nez Percé, Pawnee, Plains-

Cree, Ponca, Santee, Teton, and Yankton use three poles, or a tripod foundation. For the remaining tribes, we lack data, but it seems safe to assume that they follow one or the other of these methods. The three-pole foundation gives the projecting tops of the poles a spiral appearance while the four-pole beginning tends to group them on the sides. Thus, to a practised eye, the difference is plain. The covers, ears, doors, etc., are quite similar throughout. The shapes of tipis, however, show some differences. Thus, the Cheyenne prefer a wide base in proportion to the height while the Arapaho prefer a narrow base. Again, the Crow use very long poles, the ends projecting out above like a great funnel.

It is important to note that the use of the tipi is not confined to the plains. The Ojibway along the Lakes used it, but covered it with birchbark as did also many of the Cree and tribes formerly established in eastern Canada and New England. Even the Eastern Dakota in early days used birchbark for tipi covers. A tipi-like skin-covered tent was in general use among the Indians of Labrador and westward throughout the entire Mackenzie area of Canada. To the west, the Plains tipi was found among the Nez Percé, Flathead, Cayuse, and Umatilla; to the southwest, among the Apache. It is well-nigh impossible to determine what tribes first originated this type of shelter, though a comparison of the details of structure might give some definite

Fig. 8. Setting up a Crow Tipi.
(Petzold photo.)

39

clues. Yet, one thing is clear; viz., that it was especially adapted to the roving life of the Plains tribes
when pursuing the buffalo.

Earth-Lodges. Before going further, we must
needs recall that the tipi was not the only type of
shelter used by these Indians. The Mandan, Hidatsa, and Arikara lived in more or less permanent
villages of curious earth-covered lodges. The following description of a Hidatsa house may serve as
a type:—

On the site of a proposed lodge, they often dig down a foot or more
in order to find earth compact enough to form a good floor; so, in
some lodges, the floors are lower than the general surface of the
ground on which the village stands. The floor is of earth, and has in
its center a circular depression, for a fire-place, about a foot deep,
and three or four feet wide, with an edging of flat rocks. These
dwellings, being from thirty to forty feet in diameter, from ten to
fifteen feet high in the center, and from five to seven feet high at the
eaves, are quite commodious.

The frame of a lodge is thus made:—A number of stout posts, from
ten to fifteen, according to the size of the lodge, and rising to the
height of about five feet above the surface of the earth, are set about
ten feet apart in a circle. On the tops of these posts, solid beams
are laid, extending from one to another. Then, toward the center of
the lodge, four more posts are erected, of much greater diameter than
the outer posts, and rising to the height of ten or more feet above
the ground. These four posts stand in the corners of a square of
about fifteen feet, and their tops are connected with four heavy logs
or beams laid horizontally. From the four central beams to the
smaller external beams, long poles, as rafters, are stretched at an
angle of about 30° with the horizon; and from the outer beams to
the earth a number of shorter poles are laid at an angle of about 45°.
Finally a number of saplings or rails are laid horizontally to cover the
space between the four central beams, leaving only a hole for the
combined skylight and chimney. This frame is then covered with
willows, hay, and earth, as before mentioned; the covering being of
equal depth over all parts of the frame. (Matthews, 4–5.)

Houses of approximately the same type were used by the Pawnee, Omaha, Ponca, Kansa, Missouri, and Oto. The Osage, on the other hand, are credited with the use of dome-shaped houses covered with mats and bark, like the Ojibway and other Woodland

Fig. 9. Hidatsa Village in 1868.
(The low earth-covered lodges are obscured by the poles of drying-frames. Morrow photo reproduced by F. N. Wilson.)

tribes. The Hidatsa type of lodge is, unlike the tipi, definitely localized along the Missouri and the Platte, giving one the impression that it must have originated within this territory. The Omaha claim to have originally used tipis and to have learned the use of earth-lodges from the Arikara; likewise the

Skidi-Pawnee claim the tipi as formerly their own dwelling. However, all these tribes used tipis when on summer and winter trips after buffalo (p. 21).

Some of the Eastern Dakota lived for a part of the year in rectangular cabins of bark and poles as did some of the Woodland tribes. On the west, an oval or conical brush or grass shelter seems to have preceded the tipi. The Comanche were seen using both this western type of brush lodge and the tipi in 1853. The Northern Shoshoni have also been observed with brush lodges and tipis in the same camp. These instances are probably examples of a transition in culture. Thus, we see how even among the less civilized peoples all are prone to be influenced by the culture of their neighbors and that, in consequence, cultures grade into one another according to geographical relations.

Another curious thing is that all the tribes raising maize used earth or bark houses, but as a rule lived in them only while planting, tending, and harvesting the crop. At other times, they took to tipis. Even in mid-winter the Omaha and Eastern Dakota lived in tipis.

A unique and exceptional type of shelter was used by the Wichita and the related Caddoan tribes of the Southeastern culture area. This is known as a grass lodge. It consists of a dome-shaped structure of poles thatched with grass and given an ornamental appearance by the regular spacing of extra bunches of thatch. Formerly, each of these houses had four doors, east, west, north, and south, and four poles projected from the roof in the respective directions.

Dress. The men of the Plains were not elaborately clothed. At home, they usually went about in breech-cloth and moccasins. The former was a broad strip of cloth drawn up between the legs and passed under the belt both behind and before. There is some reason for believing that even this was introduced by white traders, the more primitive form being a small apron of dressed skin. At all seasons a man kept at hand a soft tanned buffalo robe in which he tastefully swathed his person when appearing in public. This was universally true of all, with the possible exception of some southern tribes. In the Plateau area, the most common for winter were robes of antelope, elk, and mountain sheep, while in summer elkskins without the hair were worn. Beaver skins and those of other small animals were sometimes pieced together. According to Grinnell, the Blackfoot, east of the Rocky Mountains, also used these various forms of robes. Again, the Plateau tribes sometimes used a curious woven blanket of strips of rabbitskin also widely used in Canada and the Southwest. So far this type of blanket has not been reported for the Plains tribes east of the mountains.

Everywhere, we find no differences between the robes of men and women except in their decorations. The buffalo robes were usually the entire skins with

the tail. Among most tribes, this robe was worn
horizontally with the tail on the right hand side.
Light, durable, and gaily colored blankets were later

 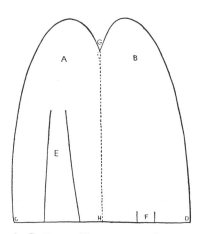

Fig. 10. One-piece Moccasin Pattern. That part of the pattern
marked *a* forms the upper side of the moccasin; *b*, the sole; *e*, the
tongue; *f*, the trailer. The leather is folded lengthwise, along the
dotted line, the points *c* and *d* are brought together and the edges
sewed along to the point *g*, which makes a seam the whole length of
the foot and around the toes. The vertical heel seam is formed by
sewing *c* and *d* now joined to *h*, *f* projecting. The strips *c* and *d* are
each half the width of that marked h, consequently the side seam at
the heel is half way between the top of the moccasin and the sole,
but reaches the level at the toes. As the sides of this moccasin are
not high enough for the wearer's comfort, an extension or ankle flap
is sewed on, varying from two to six inches in width, cut long enough
to overlap in front and held in place by means of the usual draw-
string or lacing around the ankle.

introduced by traders and are even now in general
use.

Moccasins were worn by all, the sandals of the
Southwest and Mexico not being credited to these

Indians. The two general structural types of moccasins in North America are the one-piece, or soft-
soled moccasin, and the two-piece, or hard-soled.
The latter prevails among these Indians, while the
former is general among forest Indians. A Black-

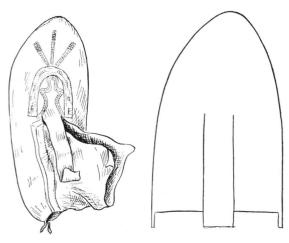

Fig. 11. Two-piece Moccasin Pattern. This type prevails in the
Plains. The soles are of stiff rawhide. They conform generally to the
outlines of the foot. The uppers are cut as shown in the patterns
though sometimes the tongue is separate. An ankle flap is added.

foot moccasin of a simple two-piece pattern is shown
in Fig. 11. The upper is made of soft tanned skin
and after finishing and decorating is sewed to a rawhide sole cut to fit the foot of the wearer. A top, or
vamp, may be added.

The pattern for a Blackfoot one-piece moccasin is
shown in Fig. 10. Our collections show that this
type occurs occasionally among the Sarsi, Blackfoot,

Plains-Cree, Assiniboin, Gros Ventre, Northern Shoshoni, Omaha, Pawnee, and Eastern Dakota. So
far, it has not been reported for any of the southern
tribes. Among many of the foregoing, this form
seems to have been preferred for winter wear, using
buffalo skin with the hair inside. Again, since all
the tribes to the north and east of these Indians
used the one-piece moccasin all the year round, its
presence in this part of the Plains is quite natural.

To the south, we find a combined stiff-soled moccasin and legging to be seen among the Arapaho,
Ute, and Comanche. This again seems to be related
to a boot type of moccasin found in parts of the
Southwest.

So, in general, the hard-soled moccasin is the type
for these Indians. Old frontiersmen claim that
from the tracks of a war party, the tribe could be
determined; this is in a measure true, for each had
some distinguishing secondary feature, such as heel
fringes, toe forms, etc., that left their marks in the
dust of the trail. Ornaments and decoration will,
however, be discussed under another head.

Almost everywhere the men wore long leggings
tied to the belt. Women's leggings were short, extending from the ankle to the knee and supported by
garters.

Some of the most conspicuous objects in the collections are the so-called war, or scalp shirts, Fig. 12.
One of the oldest was obtained by Col. Sword in
1838 and seems to be Dakota (Sioux). It is of deer-

skin. Some fine examples are credited to the Teton-
Dakota, Crow, and Blackfoot, though almost every
tribe had them in late years. This type, however,

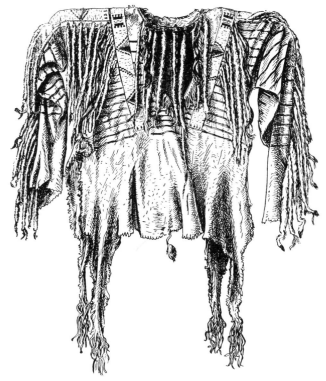

Fig. 12. Man's Shirt. Blackfoot.

should not be taken as a regular costume. Though
in quite recent years it has become a kind of tuxedo,
it was formerly the more or less exclusive uniform
of important functionaries. On the other hand, the
shirt itself, stripped of its ornaments and accesso-

Fig. 13. Costumed Figure of a Dakota Woman.

ries, seems to be of the precise pattern once worn in daily routine. Yet, the indications are that as a regular costume, the shirt was by no means in general use. The Cree, Déné, and other tribes of central Canada wore leather shirts, no doubt because of the severe winters. We also have positive knowledge of their early use by the Blackfoot, Assiniboin, Crow, Dakota, Plains-Cree, Nez Percé, Northern Shoshoni, Gros Ventre, and on the other hand of their absence among the Mandan, Hidatsa, Arikara, Pawnee, Osage, Kiowa, Cheyenne, Arapaho, and Comanche. Thus, the common shirt was after all not typical of the Plains Indians: it is only recently that the special decorated form so characteristic of the Assiniboin, Crow, Blackfoot, and Dakota has come into general use. Several interesting points may be noted in the detailed structure of these shirts, but we must pass on.

For the head there was no special covering. Yet in winter the Blackfoot, Plains-Cree, and perhaps others in the north often wore fur caps. In the south and west the head was bare, but the eyes were sometimes protected by simple shades of rawhide. So, in general, both sexes in the Plains went bareheaded, though the robe was often pulled up forming a kind of temporary hood.

Mittens and gloves seem to have been introduced by the whites, though they appear to have been native in other parts of the continent.

The women of all tribes wore more clothing than

the men.   The most typical garment was the sleeve-
less dress, a one-piece garment, an excellent example
of which is to be seen in the Audubon collection, Fig.
14.   This type was used by the Hidatsa, Mandan,

Fig. 14.   Woman's Dress of Elkskin.   Audubon.

Crow, Dakota, Arapaho, Ute, Kiowa, Comanche,
Sarsi, Gros Ventre, Assiniboin, and perhaps others.
A slight variant is reported for the Nez Percé,

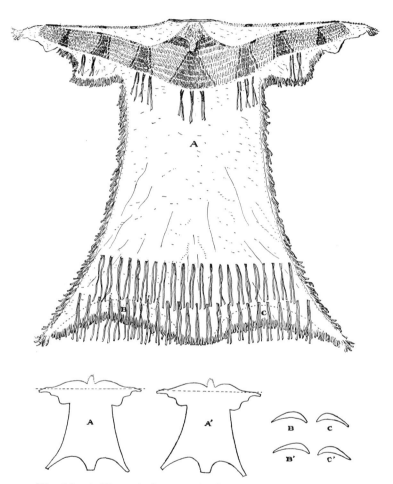

Fig. 15. A Woman's Dress made from Two Deerskins (A, A')
folded and pieced (B, C, B', C'). The skins are folded on the dotted
line and sewed together, leaving a hole for the head.

Northern Shoshoni, and Plains-Cree in that the extensions of the cape are formed into a tight-fitting sleeve. Some writers claim that in early days the Assiniboin and Blackfoot women also used this form. Formerly, the Cheyenne, Osage, and Pawnee women wore a two-piece garment consisting of a skirt and a cape, a form typical of the Woodland Indians of the east.

A close study of Plains costumes will disclose that in spite of one general pattern, there are tribal styles. In the first place, all dresses show the same main outline, curious open hanging sleeves, and a bottom of four appendages of which those at the sides are longest (Fig. 14). Almost without exception these dresses are made of two elkskins, the natural contour of which is shown in Fig. 15. The sewing of these together gives the pattern of the garment, which is modified by trimming or piecing the edges as the tribal style may require. This is a particularly good example of how the form of a costume may be determined by the material. The distribution of tribal variations in these dress patterns is shown in Fig. 16.

The shirts for men are also made of two deerskins on a slightly different pattern, but one in which the natural contour of the skin is the determining factor.

The manner of dressing the hair is often a conspicuous conventional feature. Many of the Plains tribes wore it uncropped. Among the northern tribes the men frequently gathered the hair in two

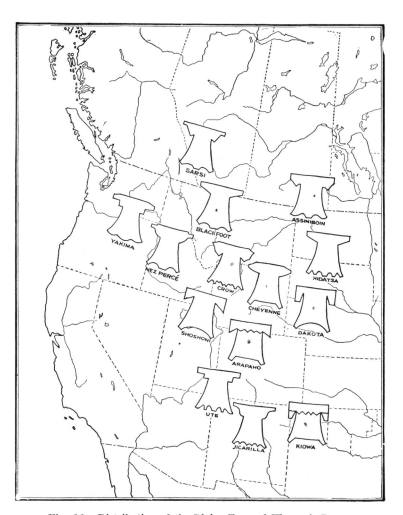

Fig. 16. Distribution of the Plains Type of Woman's Dress.

braids but in the extreme west and among some of the southern tribes, both sexes usually wore it loose on the shoulders and back. The Crow men sometimes cropped the forelock and trained it to stand erect; the Blackfoot, Assiniboin, Yankton-Dakota, Hidatsa, Mandan, Arikara, and Kiowa trained a forelock to hang down over the nose. Early writers report a general practice of artificially lengthening men's hair by gumming on extra strands until it sometimes dragged on the ground.

The hair of women throughout the Plains was usually worn in the two-braid fashion with the median part from the forehead to the neck. Old women frequently allowed the hair to hang down at the sides or confined it by a simple headband.

Again, we find exceptions in that the Oto, Osage, Pawnee, and Omaha closely cropped the sides of the head, leaving a ridge or tuft across the crown and down behind. It is almost certain that the Ponca once followed the same style and there is a tradition among the Oglala division of the Teton-Dakota that they also shaved the sides of the head. (See also History of the Expedition of Lewis and Clark, Reprinted, New York, 1902, Vol. 1, p. 135.) We may say then that the love of long heavy tresses was a typical trait of the Plains.

By the public every Indian is expected to have his hair thickly decked with feathers. The striking feather bonnets with long tails usually seen in pictures were exceptional and formerly permitted only to a few distinguished men. They are most characteristic of the Dakota. Even a common eagle feather in the hair of a Dakota had some military significance according to its form and position. On the other hand, objects tied in a Blackfoot's hair were almost certain to have a charm value. So far as we know, among all tribes, objects placed in the hair of men usually had more than a mere aesthetic significance.

Beads for the neck, ear ornaments, necklaces of claws, scarfs of otter and other fur, etc., were in general use. The face and exposed parts of the body were usually painted and sometimes the hair also. Women were fond of tracing the part line with vermilion. There was little tattooing and noses were seldom pierced. The ears, on the other hand, were usually perforated and adorned with pendants which among Dakota women were often long strings of shells reaching the waist line.

Instead of combs, brushes made from the tails of porcupines were used in dressing the hair. The most common form was made by stretching the porcupine tail over a stick of wood. The hair of the face and others parts of the body was pulled out by small tweezers.

Industrial Arts. Under this head the reader may be reminded that among most American tribes each family produces and manufactures for itself. There is a more or less definite division between the work of men and women, but beyond that there is

little specialization. The individuals are not of
equal skill, but still each practises practically the
whole gamut of industrial arts peculiar to his sex.

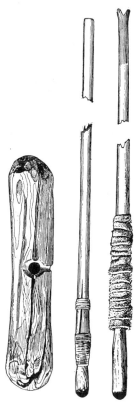

This fact greatly increases
the importance of such arts
when considered as cultural
traits.

Fire-making. The methods .of making fire are often
of great cultural interest.
So far as our data go, the
method in this area was by
the simple firedrill as shown
in the Shoshoni collections,
Fig. 17. Some of the Woodland tribes used the bowdrill
but so far this has not been
reported for the Plains. It
may be well to note that to
strike fire with flint one must
have some form of iron and
while pyrites was used by
some Eskimo and other tribes
of the far north, it seems to
have been unknown in the
Plains. Naturally, flint and
steel were among the first

Fig. 17. Firedrill. Northern Shoshoni.

articles introduced by white traders.

Textiles and Skins. While in a general way it
is true that the Plains Indians used skins instead of

cloth and basketry, it cannot be said that they were entirely unfamiliar with the basketry art. Of true cloth, we have no trace. Blankets woven with strips of rabbit fur have been noted (p. 43) and on certain Osage war bundles we find covers coarsely woven of thick strands of buffalo hair; these are about the only traces of true weaving. On the other hand, baskets were more in evidence. The Shoshoni and Ute were rather skilful, making and using many varieties of baskets. The Nez Percé made a fine soft bag like their western neighbors. The Hidatsa, Mandan, and Arikara made a peculiar carrying basket of checker weave, and are also credited with small crude coiled baskets used in gambling games. It is believed by some students that the last were occasionally made by the Arapaho, Cheyenne, Kiowa, and Dakota. The Osage have some twined bags, or soft baskets, in which ceremonial bundles are kept, but otherwise were not given to basketry. The Omaha formerly wove scarfs and belts. On the south, the Comanche are believed to have made a few crude baskets. Woven mats were almost unknown, except the simple willow backrests used by the Blackfoot, Mandan, Cheyenne, Gros Ventre, and others. These are, after all, but citations of exceptions most pronounced among the marginal tribes, the fact being that the Plains area as a whole is singularly weak in the textile arts.

Since skins everywhere took the place of cloth, the dressing of pelts was an important industry.

It was not only woman's work but her worth and virtue were estimated by her output. Soles of moc-

Fig. 18.   Fleshing a Hide.

Fig. 19.   Using a Stone Scraper.

casins, parfleche, and other similar bags were made of stiff rawhide, the product of one of the simplest and perhaps the most primitive methods of treating skins. The uppers of moccasins, soft bags, thongs, etc., were of pliable texture, produced by a more elaborate and laborious process.

For the rawhide finish the treatment is as follows:—Shortly after the removal of a hide, it is stretched out on the ground near the tipi, hair side down, and held in place by wooden stakes or pins such as are used in staking down the covers of tipis. Clinging to the upturned flesh side of the hide are many fragments of muscular tissue, fat, and strands of connective tissue, variously blackened by coagulated blood. The first treatment is that of cleaning or fleshing. Shortly after the staking out, the surface is gone over with a fleshing tool by which the adhering flesh, etc., is raked and hacked away. This is an unpleasant and laborious process requiring more brute strength than skill. Should the hide become too dry and stiff to work well, the surface is treated with warm water. After fleshing, the hide is left to cure and bleach in the sun for some days, though it may be occasionally saturated by pouring warm water over its surface. The next thing is to work the skin down to an even thickness by scraping with an adze-like tool. The stakes are usually pulled up and the hard stiff hide laid down under a sun-shade or other shelter. Standing on the hide, the woman leans over and with a sidewise movement removes the surface in chips or shavings, the action of the tool resembling that of a hand plane. After the flesh side has received this treatment, the hide is

turned and the hair scraped away in the same manner. This completes the rawhide process and the
subsequent treatment is determined by the use to be
made of it.

Fig. 20. Scraping a Hide. Blood.

The soft-tan finish as given to buffalo and deer
hides for robes, soft bags, etc., is the same in its
initial stages as the preceding. After fleshing and
scraping, the rawhide is laid upon the ground and
the surface rubbed over with an oily compound com-

posed of brains and fat often mixed with liver.
This is usually rubbed on with the hands. Any kind
of fat may be used for this purpose though the preferred substance is as stated above. The writer
observed several instances in which mixtures of
packing house lard, baking flour, and warm water
were rubbed over the rawhide as a substitute. The
rawhide is placed in the sun, after the fatty compound has been thoroughly worked into the texture
by rubbing with a smooth stone that the heat may
aid in its further distribution. When quite dry, the
hide is saturated with warm water and for a time
kept rolled up in a bundle. In this state, it usually
shrinks and requires a great deal of stretching to
get it back to its approximate former size. This is
accomplished by pulling with the hands and feet,
two persons being required to handle a large skin.
After this, come the rubbing and drying processes.
The surface is vigorously rubbed with a rough-edged
stone until it presents a clean-grained appearance.
The skin is further dried and whitened by sawing
back and forth through a loop of twisted sinew or
thong tied to the under side of an inclined tipi pole.
This friction develops considerable heat, thereby
drying and softening the texture. As this and the
preceding rubbing are parts of the same process
their chronological relation is not absolute, but the
usual order was as given above. The skin is then
ready for use.

Skins with the hair on are treated in the same

manner as above, except that the adze-tool is not applied to the hair side. A large buffalo robe was no light object and was handled with some difficulty, especially in the stretching, in consequence of which they were sometimes split down the middle and afterwards sewed together again.

Among some of the Village tribes, it seems to have been customary to stretch the skin on a four-sided frame and place it upright as shown in the exhibit for the Thompson Indians (south side of the Jesup North Pacific Hall). The exact distribution of this trait is not known but it has been credited to the Eastern Dakota, Hidatsa, and Mandan. The Blackfoot sometimes used it in winter, but laid flat upon the ground.

Buckskin was prepared in the same manner as among the forest tribes. The tribes of the western plains were especially skilful in coloring the finished skin by smoking. There were many slight variations in all the above processes.

The adze-like scraper was in general use throughout the Plains and occurs elsewhere only among bordering tribes. Hence, it is peculiar to the buffalo hunting tribes. The handle was of antler, though occasionally of wood, and the blade of iron. Information from some Blackfoot and Dakota Indians indicates that in former times the blades were of chipped stone, but the chipped scraper found in archaeological collections from the Plains area cannot be fastened to the handle in the same manner as the iron blades, the latter being placed on the inner, or under side, while the shape of the chipped stone blade seems to indicate that it was placed on the outside. Hence, the former use of stone blades for these scrapers must be considered doubtful. The iron blades are bound to the wedge-shaped haft,

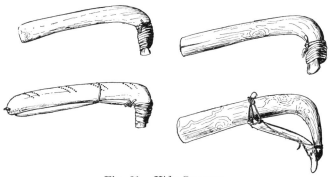

Fig. 21.   Hide Scrapers.

which each downward blow, when the tool is in use, forces tightly into the binding. When the pressure is removed the blade and binding may slip off. To prevent this, some tools are provided with a cord running from the end of the handle once or twice around its middle and thence to the binding of the blade. Again a curved iron blade is used, one end of which is bound near the middle of the handle. These types (Fig. 21) are widely distributed throughout the Plains, but the curved iron blade seems to be most frequent among the Arapaho and Cheyenne, and wooden handles among the Comanche.

On the other hand, fleshing tools, chisel-shaped
with notched edges, were used throughout Canada
east of the Rocky Mountains, and in many parts of
the United States. Hence, they cannot be taken as

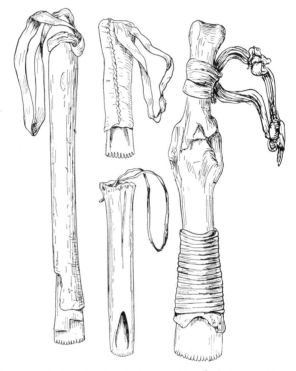

Fig. 22. Fleshing Tools. (The two short fleshers are of bone; the
one on the left is of iron; and that on the right, of bone, with an iron
blade.)

peculiar to the Plains. The older type of flesher is
apparently the one made entirely of bone, while the
later ones were made entirely of iron. Sometimes

an intermediate form is found in which a small metal blade is fastened to the end of a bone shaft (Fig. 22). The shaft of the flesher is usually covered with rawhide and to its end is attached a loop for the wrist. The iron flesher seems to be the only type peculiar to the Indians of the Plains. The distribution of the bone flesher is such that its most probable origin may be assigned to the Algonkin tribes of the Great Lakes and northward.

The production of soft buckskin usually necessitates a peculiar process called beaming, in which the skin is laid over the rounded surface of a tree section and scraped with a tool suggesting a drawshave. Beaming tools are thus identified with the dressing of deerskins and in this respect stand distinct from the adze-tool used in dressing buffalo skins. They seem to be used wherever the dressing of deerskins is prevalent and are best known under the following types:—a, split leg bones; b, combined tibia and fibula of deer or similar animal; c, rib bone; d, wooden stick with metal blade in middle, stick usually curved.

From the collections in this Museum it seems that the split leg bone type is not found in the Plains. Should further inquiry show this to be the case, it would be a matter of some interest since the split bone type is found in archaeological collections from British Columbia, Ohio, and New York, and is therefore of great antiquity as well as wide distribution. In any case the data for historic times indicate that

some form of beaming tool is a concomitant of deer-
skin dressing from Alaska and California (the
Hupa) to Labrador, and Pennsylvania.

The rubbing with a rough stone is the usual treatment accorded deerskins, and cannot be considered
peculiar to the Indians of the Plains.

Tailoring. The garments of the Indians of the
Plains were simple in construction, and the cutting
of the garment was characterized by an effort to
make the natural shape of the tanned skin fit into
the desired garment, with as little waste as possible.
(Fig. 15.) We do not know how skins were cut before the introduction of metal knives by white traders. Needles were not used by the women among
the Plains Indians, but the thread was pushed
through holes made with bodkins or awls. In
former times these awls were made of bone; the
sewing was with sinew thread made by shredding
out the long tendons from the leg of the buffalo and
deer. When sewing, Blackfoot women had at hand
a piece of dried tendon from which they pulled the
shreds with their teeth, softened them in their
mouths and then twisted them into a thread by rolling between the palms of their hands. The moisten-
ing of the sinew in the mouth not only enabled the
women to twist the thread tightly, but also caused
the sinew to expand so that when it dried in the
stitch it shrank and drew the stitches tight. The
woman's ordinary sewing outfit was carried in a
soft bag of buffalo skin and consisted of bodkins, a

piece of sinew, and a knife. Bodkins were sometimes carried in small beaded cases as shown in the
exhibit.

The Use of Rawhide. In the use of rawhide for
binding and hafting, the Plains tribes seem almost
unique. When making mauls and stone-headed
clubs a piece of green or wet hide is firmly sewed on
and as this dries its natural shrinkage sets the parts
firmly. This is nicely illustrated in saddles. Thus,
rawhide here takes the place of nails, twine, cement,
etc., in other cultures.

The Parfleche. A number of characteristic bags
were made of rawhide, the most conspicuous being
the parfleche. Its simplicity of construction is in-
spiring and its usefulness scarcely to be over-esti-
mated. The approximate form for a parfleche is
shown in Fig. 23, and its completed form in Fig. 24.
The side outlines as in Fig. 23 are irregular and
show great variations, none of which can be taken
as certainly characteristic. To fill the parfleche, it
is opened out as in Fig. 23, and the contents arranged in the middle. The large flap is then brought
over and held by lacing a′, a″. The ends are then
turned over and laced, b′, b″. The closed parfleche
may then be secured by both or either of the looped
thongs at c′, c″.

Primarily, parfleche were used for holding dried
meat, dried berries, tallow, etc., though utensils and
other belongings found their way into them when
convenient. In recent years, they seem to have

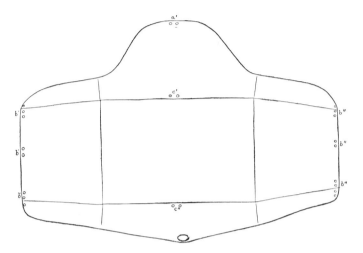

Fig. 23.   Parfleche Pattern.

Fig. 24.   A Parfleche.

more of a decorative than a practical value; or rather, according to our impression, they are cherished as mementos of buffalo days, the great good old time of Indian memory, always appropriate and

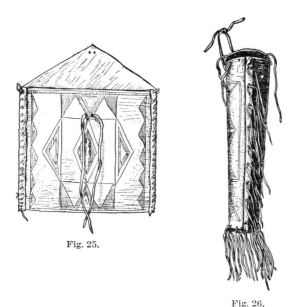

Fig. 25.

Fig. 26.

Fig. 25. Bag made of Rawhide.
Fig. 26. A Case made of Rawhide.

acceptable as gifts. The usual fate of a gift parfleche is to be cut into moccasin soles. With the possible exception of the Osage, the parfleche was common among all these tribes but seldom encountered elsewhere.

Rawhide Bags. A rectangular bag (Fig. 25) was also common and quite uniform even to the modes of binding. They were used by women rather than by men. The larger ones may contain skin-dressing tools, the smaller ones, sewing or other small implements, etc. Sometimes, they were used in gather-

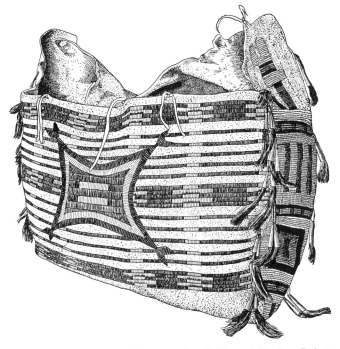

Fig. 27. Bag decorated with Porcupine Quills and Beads. Dakota.

ing berries and other vegetable foods. A cylindrical rawhide case used for headdresses and other ceremonial objects is characteristic (Fig. 26). All these objects made of rawhide are further characterized by their highly individualized painted decorations (p. 132).

Soft Bags. The Dakota made some picturesque soft bags, used in pairs, and called ''A bag for every possible thing.'' The collection contains many fine

Fig. 28. Pipe and Tobacco Bags. Dakota.

examples some of which are of buffalo hide. All are skilfully decorated with quills or beads (Fig. 27). This type occurs among the Assiniboin, Gros Ventre, Dakota, Crow, Cheyenne, Arapaho, Ute, and Wind

River Shoshoni in almost identical forms, but among the Nez Percé and Bannock with decided differences.

Perhaps equally typical of the area were the long slender bags for smoking outfits. These are especially conspicuous in Dakota collections where they range from 80 to 150 cm. in length. At the ends, they have rows of rawhide strips wrapped with quills and below a fringe of buckskin (Fig. 28). The Dakota type has been noted among the Assiniboin, Cheyenne, Crow, and Hidatsa, but rarely among the Ute, Arapaho, or Shoshoni. The Kiowa and Comanche make one, but with an entirely different fringe. The Blackfoot, Northern Shoshoni, Plains-Cree, and Sarsi use a smaller pouch of quite a different type, also reported from the Saulteaux and Cree of the Woodland area. These objects are, however, so often presented to visiting Indians that collectors find it difficult to separate the intrusions from the native samples for any particular tribe.

We have some reason for thinking that the Dakota type is quite recent, for the Teton claim that formerly the entire skins of young antelope, deer, and even birds and beavers were used as smoking bags. Some examples of such bags have been collected and are quite frequent in the ceremonial outfits of the Blackfoot. Again, the collections from many tribes contain bags made from the whole skins of unborn buffalo and deer, used for gathering berries and storing dried food, from which it is clear that a general type of seamless bag was once widely used. All this raises the question as to whether the introduction of metal cutting and sewing implements during the historic period may not have influenced the development of these long, rectangular fringed pipe bags.

The strike-a-light pouch often made of modern commercial leather is common to the Wind River Shoshoni, Ute, Arapaho, Cheyenne, Dakota, Gros

Fig. 29. Strike-a-light Pouch. Arapaho.

Ventre, and Assiniboin (Fig. 29). Among the Arapaho and Gros Ventre we also find a large pouch of similar designs. Again, the Northern Shoshoni and Blackfoot are not included, neither are these pouches frequent among the Kiowa and Comanche.

Many of the paint bags used by the Blackfoot resemble their pipe bags even to the fringe and the flaps at the mouth. However, many paint bags in ceremonial outfits are without fringes or decorations of any kind. Some have square cut bases and some curved; their lengths range from 8 to 15 cm. In

some cases, those with square cut bases are provided
with a pendant at each corner. Decorated paint
bags of the fringed type occur among the Gros
Ventre, Assiniboin, Arapaho, Sarsi, Dakota, and
Shoshoni. A specimen without the fringe appears
in the Comanche collection. The Blackfoot, Sarsi,
Gros Ventre, and Assiniboin use almost exclusively
bags with the flaps at the top, and bearing similar
decorations. The Arapaho and Dakota incline to
this type but also use those with straight tops.
Among the Shoshoni decorated paint bags are rare,
but two specimens we have observed belong to these
respective types. So far, it seems that the Arapaho
alone use the peculiar paint bag with a triangular
tail, suggesting the ornamented pendants to the animal skin medicine bags of the Algonkin in the Woodland area. However, we have seen a large bag of
this pattern attributed to the Bannock.

A round-bottomed pouch with a decorated field
and a transverse fringe was sometimes used for
paint by the Blackfoot. The decorated part is on
stiff rawhide while the upper is of soft leather, the
sides and mouth of which are edged by two and three
rows of beads respectively. This seems to be an
unusual form for the Blackfoot and rare in other
collections; while the related form, a large rounded
bag, frequently encountered in Dakota and Assiniboin collections, has not been observed among the
northern group of tribes. The Blackfoot collection
contains two small, flat rectangular cases with

fringes. One of these was said to have been made for a mirror, the other for matches. However, such cases were formerly used by many tribes for carrying the ration ticket issued by the government. Their distribution seems to have been general in the Plains.

Some tribes used a long double saddle bag, highly decorated and fringed. There was usually a slit at one side for the horn of the saddle. So far, these have been reported for the Blackfoot, Sarsi, Crow, Dakota, and Cheyenne. They are mentioned as common in the Missouri area by Larpenteur, who implies that the shape is copied after those used by whites. Morice credits the Carrier of the Mackenzie culture area with similar bags used on dogs.

It will be noted that in style and range of bags and pouches, the Village group of these Indians (p. 19) tends to stand apart from the other groups much more distinctly than the intermediate tribes of the west, for between the latter and the typical Plains tribes there are few marked differences.

Household Utensils. In a preceding section, reference was made to baskets which, in parts of the Plateau area on the west, often served as pots for boiling food. They were not, of course, set upon the fire, the water within being heated by hot stones. Pottery was made by the Hidatsa, Mandan, and Arikara, and probably by all the other tribes of the Village group. There is some historical evidence that it was once made by the Blackfoot and there are traditions of its use among the Gros Ventre, Cheyenne, and Assiniboin; but, with the possible exception of the Blackfoot, it has not been definitely credited to any of the nine typical tribes.

We have no definite information as to how foods were boiled among these non-pottery making tribes before traders introduced kettles. Many tribes, however, knew how to hang a fresh paunch upon sticks and boil in it with stones (Fig. 30). Some used a fresh skin in a hole. Thus Catlin says:—

There is a very curious custom amongst the Assinneboins, from which they have taken their name; a name given them by their neighbors, from a singular mode they have of boiling their meat, which is done in the following manner:—when they kill meat, a hole is dug in the ground about the size of a common pot, and a piece of the raw hide of the animal, as taken from the back, is put over the hole, and then pressed down with the hands close around the sides, and filled with water. The meat to be boiled is then put in this hole or pot of water; and in a fire which is built near by, several large stones are heated to a red heat, which are successively dipped and held in the water until the meat is boiled; from which singular and peculiar custom, the Ojibbeways have given them the appellation of Assinneboins or stone boilers.

The Traders have recently supplied these people with pots; and even long before that, the Mandans had instructed them in the secret of manufacturing very good and serviceable earthen pots; which together have entirely done away [with] the custom, excepting at public festivals; where they seem, like all others of the human family, to take pleasure in cherishing and perpetuating their ancient customs. (p. 54.)

These methods were known to the Arapaho, Crow, Dakota, Gros Ventre, Blackfoot, and Assiniboin. Doubtless they were generally practised elsewhere in the Plains. Since California and the whole Pa-

cific coast northward as well as the interior plateaus
had stone-boiling as a general cultural trait, this distribution in the Plains is easily accounted for.   On

Fig. 30.   Boiling with Hot Stones in a Paunch supported by Sticks.
Blackfoot.

the other hand, the eastern United States appears
as a great pottery area whose influence reached the
Village tribes.

So, excepting the pottery-making Village tribes, the methods of cooking in the Plains area before traders introduced kettles seem to have comprised broiling over the fire, baking in holes in the ground, and boiling in vessels of skin, basketry, or bark. For the first, pieces of meat were impaled on a stick

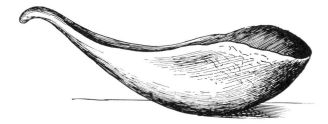

Fig. 31. Buffalo Horn Spoon.

and either held over the fire or the butt of the stick thrust in the ground. Cooking in a hole was universal in the basin of the Columbia River, especially for edible roots. A pit was dug and a fire built in and over it. When a great mass of embers and ashes had accumulated they were scraped away, the hole lined with leaves or bark, the roots put in and covered, after which the ashes and embers were scraped over all. After the proper interval the pit was opened and the food served. The tribes on the western border of the Plains, the Blackfoot, Shoshoni, etc., also cooked roots in this way, but in common with the typical tribes used the same method for meat. Thus we see that neither pottery nor metal vessels are essential to good cooking.

Buffalo horn spoons were used by all and whenever available ladles and dishes were fashioned from mountain sheep horn. Those of buffalo horn were used in eating; those of mountain sheep horn usually for dipping, skimming and other culinary processes. In making these spoons, the horn was generally scorched over a fire until some of the gluey matter tried out, and then trimmed to the desired shape with a knife. Next it was boiled in water until soft, when the bowl was shaped over a water-worn stone of suitable size and the handle bent into the proper shape. The sizes and forms of such spoons varied a great deal, but no important tribal differences have been observed. In traveling, spoons, as well as bowls, were usually carried in bags of buffalo skin. Among the Village tribes, wooden spoons were common, similar to those from Woodland collections. Bowls were fashioned from wood but were rare among the southern and western tribes. Knots of birch and other hard wood found occasionally along rivers were usually used for bowls. These were worked into shape by burning, scraping down with bits of stone, and finally polishing. They were used in eating, each person usually owning one which he carried with him when invited to a feast. Occasionally, bowls were made of mountain sheep horn; but such were the exception, rather than the rule. The finest bowls seem to have been made by the Dakota, and the crudest by the Comanche and Ute.

Tools. It is believed that formerly knives were made of bone and stone, but we have no very definite data. In fact, many tribes secured knives and other trade articles by barter with other Indians long before they were visited by explorers; hence, we have little in the way of historical data.

Some years ago a Museum field-worker chanced upon an old blind man smoothing down a walking stick with a stone flake, an interesting survival of primitive life. We can scarcely realize how quickly the civilized trader changed the material culture of the Indians. Perrot, one of the first French explorers visiting the eastern border of this area, gives the following report of an address he made to some Fox and other Indians, "I see this fine village filled with young men, who are, I am sure, as courageous as they are well built; and who will, without doubt, not fear their enemies if they carry French weapons. It is for these young men that I leave my gun, which they must regard as the pledge of my esteem for their valor; they must use it if they are attacked. It will also be more satisfactory in hunting cattle [buffalo] and other animals than are all the arrows that you use. To you who are old men I leave my kettle; I carry it everywhere without fear of breaking it. You will cook in it the meat that your young men bring from the chase, and the food which you offer to the Frenchmen who come to visit you." He tossed a dozen awls and knives to the women, and said to them: "Throw aside your bone bodkins;

these French awls will be much easier to use. These
knives will be more useful to you in killing beavers
and in cutting your meat than are the pieces of
stone that you use.'' Then, throwing to them some
rassade (beads): ''See; these will better adorn your
children and girls than do their usual ornaments''
(p. 330). This is a fair sample of what occurred
everywhere. On the other hand, the Indian did not
so readily change his art, religion, and social customs.

Perhaps the best early observer of primitive tools
was Captain Lewis who writes of the Northern Shoshoni in the Original Journals of the Lewis and
Clark Expedition, Vol. 3, p. 19, as follows:—

> The metal which we found in possession of these people consisted
> of a few indifferent knives, a few brass kettles some arm bands of
> iron and brass, a few buttons, woarn as ornaments in their hair, a
> spear or two of a foot in length and some iron and brass arrow points
> which they informed me they obtained in exchange for horses from
> the Crow or Rocky Mountain Indians on the yellowstone River. the
> bridlebits and stirreps they obtained from the Spaniards, tho these
> were but few, many of them made use of flint for knives, and with
> this instrument, skined the animals they killed, dressed their fish and
> made their arrows; this flint is of no regular form, and if they can
> only obtain a part of it, an inch or two in length that will cut they
> are satisfyed. they renew the edge by flecking off the flint by means
> of the point of an Elk's or deer's horn. with the point of a deer or
> Elk's horn they also form their arrow points of the flint, with a
> quickness and neatness that is really astonishing. we found no axes
> nor hatchets among them; what wood they cut was done either with
> stone or Elk's horn. the latter they use always to rive or split their
> wood.

Among the collections from the Blackfoot and
Gros Ventre, we find models of bone knives made by

old people who claimed to have used such (Fig. 32).
There are also a few flakes of stone said to have been
so used when metal knives were not at hand.

Fig. 32.   Bone Knife.

No aboriginal axes have been preserved but they
are said to have been made of stone and bone.   The
hafted stone maul (Fig. 4) is everywhere present
and we are told that the ax was hafted in a similar
manner.   Drilling was performed with arrow points
and wood was dressed by stone scrapers.

Though we may be sure that the tribes of the
Plains were, like those in most parts of prehistoric
America, living in a stone age at the time of discovery, it is probable that they made some use of
copper.   The eastern camps of the Eastern Dakota
were near the copper mines of Lake Superior and
in 1661 Radisson, a famous explorer, saw copper
ornaments while among their villages in Minnesota.
Prehistoric copper implements are numerous in
Minnesota and Wisconsin but such objects are rare
within the Plains area.   Yet, all these implements
were of pure copper and therefore too soft to displace stone and bone, the Plains Indian at all events
living in a true stone age culture.

Digging Stick. From a primitive point of view, the digging stick is most interesting. It has been reported from the Blackfoot, Gros Ventre, Hidatsa, Mandan, and Dakota as a simple pointed stick, used chiefly in digging edible roots and almost exclusively by women. (It is important to note the symbolic survival of this implement in the sun dance bundle of the Blackfoot.) Some curious agricultural implements are to be found in the Hidatsa collection, especially hoes made from the shoulder blades of buffalo. The latter have been reported from the Pawnee, Arikara, and Mandan.

Pipes. The Eastern Dakota have long been famous for the manufacture of pipes from catlinite or red pipe-stone which even in prehistoric times seems to have been distributed by trade. Some pipes in the Museum were collected in 1840 and are of the types described by Catlin and other early writers. Many of the Village tribes used pottery pipes. Among the Assiniboin, Gros Ventre, and Blackfoot, a black stone was used for a Woodland type of pipe. In the Plateau area, the pipes were smaller than elsewhere and usually made from steatite. The Hidatsa and Mandan used a curiously shaped pipe, as may be seen from the collection. It is much like the Arapaho sacred tribal flat pipe. Occasionally, a straight tubular pipe was used. Among the Cheyenne in particular, this was a bone reinforced with sinew. Also, it seems to have been generally known to the Kiowa and Arapaho. Among the Blackfoot and Dakota, it is usually a simple stone tube with a stem. This form is everywhere exceptional and usually ceremonial.

The large medicine-pipe, or ceremonial, of the Blackfoot Indians, conspicuously displayed in the hall is scarcely to be considered under this head (see p. 115), as also the curious pipe-like wands of the Dakota, the Omaha (Demuth collection), and Pawnee.

Tobacco was raised (p. 30) by a few tribes. This was mixed with the dried bark of the red willow, the leaves of the bear berry or with larb. Some wild species of *Nicotiana* were gathered by the Plateau tribes. In literature, the term *kinnikinnick* (Algonkian Ojibway, meaning "what is mixed") is applied to this mixture. From the very first, traders introduced commercial forms of tobacco which have been in general use ever since.

Weapons. Reference has been made to bows, clubs, and lances (p. 26) for killing buffalo; hence, it is only necessary to add that they were also the chief weapons in war. Among nearly all the tribes a circular shield of buffalo hide was used, though with so many ceremonial associations that it is not clear whether the Indian prized it most for its charm value or for its mechanical properties, since in most cases he seems to have placed his faith in the powers symbolized in the devices painted thereon. No armor seems to have been used. The typical Plains Indian rode into battle, stripped to breechcloth and moccasins, with whatever symbolic headgear, charms, and insignia he was entitled to. However, the Blackfoot have traditions of having protected

Fig. 33.   A Buffalo Hide Shield from the Northern Blackfoot.

themselves from arrows by several skin shirts, one over the other, while among the Northern Shoshoni, both men and horses were protected by "many folds

of dressed antelope skin united with glue and sand."
The Pawnee have also been credited with hardened
skin coats. Since armor and helmets were used in
some parts of the North Pacific Coast area and in
parts of the Plateaus, it is natural to encounter armor on the northwestern margin of the Plains.
Poisoned arrows have been credited to the Plateau
tribes and a few of those in the western Plains.

Games. Amusements and gambling are repre-
sented in collections by many curious devices.
Adults rarely played for amusement, leaving such
pastime to children; they themselves played for
stakes. Most American games are more widely distributed than many other cultural traits; but a few
seem almost entirely peculiar to the Plains.

A game in which a forked anchor-like stick is
thrown at a rolling ring was known to the Dakota,
Omaha, and Pawnee. So far, it has not been reported from other tribes.

Another game of limited distribution is the large
hoop with a double pole, the two players endeavor-
ing to place the poles so that when the hoop falls, it
will make a count according to which of the four
marks in the circumference are nearest a pole. This
has been reported for the Arapaho, Dakota, and
Omaha. Among the Dakota, this game seems to
have been associated with magical ceremonies for
"calling the buffalo" and also played a part in the
ghost dance (p. 124) movement. The Arapaho have
also a sacred hoop game associated with the sun

dance.   Other forms of this game in which a single pole is used have been reported from almost every tribe in the Plains.   It occurs also outside this area. Yet, in the Plains it takes special forms in different localities.   Thus the Blackfoot and their neighbors used a very small spoked ring with an arrow for the pole, the Mandan used a small plain ring but with a very long pole, while the Comanche used a large life-preserver-like hoop with a sectioned club for a pole.

The netted hoop at which darts were thrown is almost universal in the Plains, but occurs elsewhere as well.   Other popular games were stick dice and the hand game (hiding the button).   Among the Blackfoot and their neighbors, the hand game was a favorite gambling device and handled by team work; i.e., one large group played against another.

By a comparative study of games, it would be possible to divide the tribes of the Plains into a number of geographical subgroups.   On the other hand, it is clear that, taken as a whole, these tribes have sufficient similarities in games to justify grouping them in a distinct culture area.

We have now passed in review the main characteristics of material culture among the Plains tribes. There are many other important details having functional and comparative significance for whose consideration the reader must be referred to the special literature.   We have seen how the typical, or central, group of tribes (Blackfoot, Gros Ventre, Assiniboin, Crow, Teton-Dakota, Cheyenne, Arapaho, Kiowa, and Comanche) seems to have few traits in common with adjoining culture areas, while the border tribes manifest a mixture of the traits emphasized among the typical group and those most characteristic of other culture areas. For example, the typical material culture of the Plains is peculiar in the absence of pottery, the textile arts, agriculture, and the use of wild grains and seeds, all of which appear to varying degrees in one or the other of the marginal groups.

In general, it appears that in the Plains, traits of material culture fall within geographical rather than linguistical and political boundaries. While all cultural traits seem to show the same tendency, this is most pronounced in material culture. Thus, from the point of view of this chapter the Plains-Cree may merit a place in the typical group, but in some other respects hold an intermediate position. All the other tribes without exception manifest some important traits of material culture found in other areas.

In part the causes for the observed greater uniformity in material culture seem to lie in the geographical environment, since food, industries, and some household arts are certain to be influenced by the character of the materials available. This, however, cannot be the whole story, for pottery clay is everywhere within easy reach, yet the typical tribes were not potters. They also wanted not the opportunities to learn the art from neighboring tribes. It seems more probable that certain dominant factors in their lives exercised a selective influence over the many cultural traits offered at home and abroad, thus producing a culture well adapted to the place and to the time.

Chapter II.

SOCIAL ORGANIZATION.

MUSEUM collections cannot illustrate this important phase of culture; but since no comprehensive view of the subject can be had without its consideration, we must give it some space. It is customary to treat of all habits or customs having to do with the family organization, the community, and what we call the state, under the head of social organization. So, in order that the reader may form some general idea of social conditions in this area, we shall review some of the discussed points. Unfortunately, the data for many tribes are meager so that a complete review cannot be made. The Blackfoot, Sarsi, Crow, Northern Shoshoni, Nez Percé, Assiniboin, Teton-Dakota, Omaha, Hidatsa, Arapaho, Cheyenne, and Kiowa have been carefully investigated, but of the remaining tribes we know very little.

As previously stated, it is customary to accept the political units of the Indian as tribes or independent nations. Thus, while the Crow recognize several subdivisions, they feel that they are one people and support a council or governing body for the whole. The Blackfoot, on the other hand, are composed of three distinct political divisions, the Piegan, Blood, and Blackfoot, with no superior government, yet they feel that they are one people with common interests and, since they have a common speech and precisely similar cultures, it is customary to ignore the political units and designate them by the larger term. The Hidatsa, one of the Village group, have essentially the same language as the Crow, but have many different traits of culture and, while conscious of a relationship, do not recognize any political sympathies. Again, in the Dakota, we have a more complicated scheme. They recognize first seven divisions as "council fires"—Mdewakanton, Wahpekute, Sisseton, Yankton, Yanktonai, and Teton. These, as indicated by separate fires, were politically independent, but did not make war upon each other. To the whole, they gave the name Dakota, or "those who are our friends." Again, they grouped the first four into a larger whole, the Eastern Dakota (Isayanti), the Yankton and Yanktonai formed a second group, and the Teton a third. However, the culture of the second and third groups is so similar that it is quite admissible to include them under the title Teton-Dakota. All the seven divisions were again subdivided, especially the Teton, which had at least eight large practically independent divisions.

Thus, it is clear that no hard and fast distinctions can be made between independent and dependent political units, for in some cases the people feel as if one and yet support what seem to be separate governments. This is not by any means peculiar to the Plains. Since anthropology is, after all, chiefly a study of culture, it is usual to place under one head all units having exactly the same culture when otherwise closely related by language and blood. Our previous list of tribes, therefore, embraces groups, all subdivisions of which have approximately equal cultural values for the whole series of traits (p. 19).

Using the term tribe to designate units with independent governing bodies, we find that these tribes are in turn composed of small units, each under the leadership of a chief, seconded by a few head men. These subdivisions are often designated in technical literature as bands—a chief and his followers. It frequently happens that the members of these bands inherit their memberships according to a fixed system. When this is reckoned through the mother, or in the female line, the term clan is used instead of band; when reckoned in the male line, gens. The clans and gentes of the Plains are of special interest because of the tendency to regulate marriage so that it must be exogamic, or between individuals from different clans and gentes, and also because of the difficulty in discovering whether this is due to the mere accident of blood relationship or some other obscure tendency. On this point there is a large body of special literature.

An exogamic gentile system has been reported for the Omaha, Ponca, Iowa, Oto, Missouri, Osage, and Kansas. An exogamic clan system prevails among the Hidatsa, Crow, and the Mandan. Among the Plateau group, the Arapaho, Kiowa, Comanche, and

probably also among the Dakota and Plains-Cree, we
have only bands without marriage restrictions. In
addition, we have some problematical cases in the
Blackfoot, Gros Ventre, Assiniboin, and perhaps

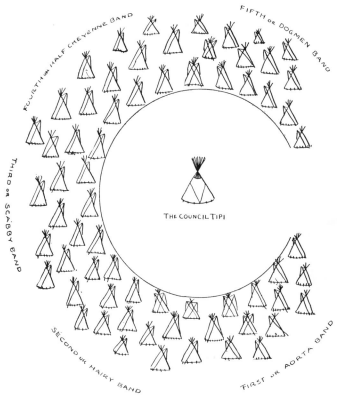

Fig. 34. The Cheyenne Camp Circle. (Dorsey.)

others, where there seems to be a tendency toward a
gentile exogamous system, but our data are not sufficiently full to determine whether these are intermediate or true transitional types.

The Camp Circle. Among the typical tribes and even in most places where tipis were used, we find an organized camp, or circle. In its pure form, this is a tribal scheme by which each "band" has a fixed place or order, generally enumerated sunwise, from the opening of the circle in the easternmost segment (Fig. 34). When forming a camp, the leaders selected the site and marked off the two sides of the opening, or gap, whence the respective bands fell in, in proper order and direction, to form the circle. At the center was a council tent, where the governing body met and at symmetrical points were the tipis of the "soldiers," or police. While the camp circle was the most striking and picturesque trait of Plains culture, it was probably no more than a convenient form of organized camp for a political group composed of "bands." It is likely that some of the typical tribes developed it first, whence, because of its practical value, it was adopted by the others and even some of the Village and Plateau tribes when they used tipis. It is, however, peculiar to the Plains.

Marriage. There seems to be nothing distinctive in the marriage customs of the Plains, even in the matter of exogamy (p. 92). A man was permitted to marry as many women as he desired, yet relatively few men had more than three wives. Everywhere the rule was to marry sisters, if possible, since it is said they were less likely to quarrel amongst themselves. As no slaves were kept and servants were unknown, the aristocratic family could only meet the situation by increasing the number of wives. Further, it was usual to regard the first wife as the head of the family, the others as subordinate.

The care and rearing of children is a universal phase of human life. Among the collections will be found cradles, or carriers, for the protection of the newly born, often highly ornamented. Dolls and miniature objects such as travois, saddles, and bags, were common as toys and often find their way into museums. A curious custom, not confined to the Plains, was to preserve the navel cord in a small ornamented pouch, hung to the cradle or about the neck of the child. Among the Dakota, these usually took the forms of turtles and lizards, among the Blackfoot, snakes and horned toads, etc. Examples are shown in the various collections.

Naming children is everywhere an important matter. Usually an old person is called in to do this and selects a single name. When a boy reaches adolescence, a new name is often given and again, if, as an adult, he performs some meritorious deed. Girls seldom change their names, not even at marriage. Among many tribes there are special ceremonies for girls when adolescence sets in.

When an Indian is ill a doctor is called in. He is supposed to have received power from some supernatural source and sings songs and prays at the bedside. Sometimes vegetable substances are given as

medicine, but these are usually harmless, the faith
being placed entirely in the religious formula.

At death the body was dressed and painted, then
wrapped in a robe and placed upon a scaffold, in a
tree, or upon a hill. None of the Plains tribes seem
to have practised cremation and but a few of them
placed the bodies underground. In fact, the Government authorities experienced great difficulty in
inducing the modern Indians to inter their dead, as
it is against their old belief, in that it would inter-
fere with the passage of the spirit to the other world.

Government. The political organization was
rather loose and in general quite democratic. Each
band, gens, or clan informally recognized an indefinite number of men as head men, one or more of
whom were formally vested with representative
powers in the tribal council. Among the Dakota,
there was a kind of society of older men, self-elect-
ing, who legislated on all important matters. They
appointed four of their number to exercise the ex-
ecutive functions. The Omaha had a somewhat
similar system. The Cheyenne had four chiefs of
equal rank and a popularly elected council of forty
members. Among the Blackfoot we seem to have a
much less systematic arrangement, the leading men
of each band forming a general council which in turn
recognized one individual as chief. Of the western
tribes the Northern Shoshoni, at least, had even a
less formal system.

Though there were in the Plains some groups

spoken of as confederacies by pioneers; viz., the
Blackfoot, Sarsi, and Gros Ventre; the seven Dakota tribes; the Pawnee group; the Arapaho, Cheyenne, Kiowa, and Comanche, none of these seem to
have been more than alliances. At least, there was
nothing like the celebrated League of the Iroquois
in the Woodland area.

Soldier Bands or Societies. We have previously
mentioned the camp police. The Dakota governing
society, for example, appointed eight or more men
as soldiers or marshals to enforce their regulations
at all times. There were also a number of men's societies or fraternities of a military and ceremonial
character upon one or more of which the tribal government might also call for such service. As these
societies had an organization of their own, it was
only necessary to deal with their leaders. The call
to service was for specific occasions and the particular society selected automatically ceased to act when
the occasion passed. The Blackfoot, Gros Ventre,
Assiniboin, Cheyenne, Arapaho, Crow, Hidatsa,
Mandan, Arikara, and Pawnee, also had each a number of societies upon whom the governing body
called for police service. In addition to these specific parallels, we find that all tribes using the camp
circle, or organized camp, when hunting buffalo, also
appointed police who executed orders in a similar
manner. Among the tribes having soldier societies
we again find certain marked similarities in the current names for these organizations as shown in

Fig. 35. A Dog Dancer. Hidatsa. (After Maximilian.)

the following partial list, compiled by Dr. R. H.
Lowie:

Mandan	Hidatsa	Arikara	Blackfoot	Arapaho	Gros Ventre
—	Kit-foxes	Foxes	Kit-foxes	Kit-foxes	Kit-foxes
—	—	—	Mosquitoes	—	Flies
Ravens	Ravens	Crows	Ravens	—	—
Half-Shorn Heads	Half-Shorn Heads	—	—	—	—
Foolish Dogs	Crazy Dogs	Mad Dogs	Crazy Dogs	Crazy Lodge	Crazy Lodge
Dogs (?)	Small Dogs	Young Dogs	—	—	—
Old Dogs	Dogs	Big Young Dogs (?)	Dogs	Dogs	Dogs
					—
Soldiers	Enemies	Soldiers	{ Braves (?) Soldiers (?)	—	
Buffaloes	Bulls	Mad Bulls	Bulls	—	—

It will be noted that a mad or foolish society is
found in each of the six tribes as is also a dog society, while the kit-fox and the raven are common
to a number. Investigations of these organizations
have shown that though those bearing similar names
are not exact duplicates, they nevertheless have
many fundamental elements in common.

The most probable explanation of this correspondence in name and element is that each distinct society had a common origin, or that the bulls, for example, were created by one tribe and then passed on
to others. This is an important point because
among anthropologists there are two extreme the-
ories to account for similarities in culture, one that
all like cultural traits, wherever found, had a common origin, the other that all were invented or derived independently by the tribes practising them.
The former is often spoken of as the diffusion of

Fig. 36. Dance of the Bull Society. Mandan. (After Maximilian.)

100

cultural traits, the latter as independent development. It is generally agreed, however, that most cultures contain traits acquired by diffusion (or borrowing) as well as some entirely original to themselves, the whole forming a complex very difficult to analyze. Returning to these Plains Indian societies we find among several tribes (Blackfoot, Gros Ventre, Arapaho, Mandan, and Hidatsa) an additional feature in that the societies enumerated in our table are arranged in series so that ordinarily a man passes from one to the other in order, like school children in their grades, thus automatically grouping the members according to age. For this variety, the term age-society has been used by Dr. Kroeber. Thus, it appears that while in certain general features the soldier band system of police is found among all tribes in the area, there are many other interesting differences distributed to varying extents. For example, the age grouping is common to but five tribes, while among the Arapaho it takes a special form, the age grouping being combined with appropriate ceremonial, or dancing functions, including practically all the adult males in the tribes. An unusually complete set of the regalia of the Arapaho series is exhibited in the Museum and from the Gros Ventre, a related tribe, is shown the only known specimen of the peculiar shirt worn by a highest degree dog society member. Other regalia are exhibited for the Blackfoot, Crow, and Hidatsa.

Among the Blackfoot, Arapaho, Hidatsa, Mandan, and Gros Ventre, we find one or more women's societies not in any way performing police functions, but still regarded as somehow correlated with the series for men. Among the Blackfoot and Arapaho, the one women's society is based upon mythical conceptions of the buffalo as is illustrated by their re-

Fig. 37.   Headdress of Buffalo Skin.   Arapaho Women's Society.

galia (Fig. 37). Among the Mandan, where there were several women's societies, we may note a buffalo organization whose ceremonies were believed to charm the buffalo near when game was scarce and the tribe threatened with starvation. Some of their regalia will be found in the Museum.

These societies for both men and women, in their fundamental and widely distributed features, must be set down with the camp circle as one of the most characteristic social traits of the Plains.

A careful study of the age-societies and a comparison of their essential features with the societies of other Plains tribes indicates that they originated in the Plains and were probably the original invention of the Mandan and Hidatsa. At least, we can be sure that these Village tribes were the center of distribution for Plains societies as a whole.

Social Distinction. There being no such thing as individual ownership of land, property consisted of horses, food, utensils, etc. These were possessed in varying degrees by the individual members of a tribe, but in no case was the amount of such property given much weight in the determination of social position. Anyone in need of food, horses, or anything whatsoever, was certain to receive some material assistance from those who had an abundance. Among most tribes, the lavish giving away of property was a sure road to social distinction. Yet, the real aristocrats seem to have been those with great and good deeds to their credit. The Dakota, Blackfoot, Cheyenne, and no doubt others, had a more or less definite system for the grading of war deeds, among the highest being the "coup," or the touching of an enemy. Curiously enough, this touching as well as capturing a gun was regarded by the Blackfoot, at least, as deserving of greater rank than the mere taking of an enemy's life. The Teton-Dakota, on the other hand, while recognizing

Fig. 38.   A Blackfoot War Record.   Beginning at the top, we have Bear-chief (a) on foot surprised by Assiniboin Indians but he escaped; (b) Double-runner cut loose four horses; (c) Double-runner captures a Gros Ventre boy; (d) Double-runner and a companion encounter and kill two Gros Ventre, he taking a lance from one; (e) even while a boy Double-runner picked up a war-bonnet dropped by a fleeing Gros Ventre which in the system counts as a deed; (f) as a man he has two adventures with Crow Indians, taking a gun from one; (g) he, as leader, met five Flathead in a pit and killed them; (h) a Cree took shelter in some cherry brush in a hole, but Big-nose went in for him; (i) not completely shown, but representing a Cree Indian killed while running off Piegan horses; (j) Double-runner, carrying a medicine-pipe, took a bow from a Gros Ventre and then killed him; (k) Double-runner took a shield and a horse from a Crow tipi, a dog barked and he was hotly pursued; (m) he killed two Gros Ventre and took two guns; (n) he captured a Gros Ventre woman and a boy; (o) he took four mules.

104

the high value of the coup, also put great stress on the taking of a scalp. Running off, or stealing the horses of another tribe, was also a worthy feat among all these Indians. Among most tribes, it was customary at feasts and other gatherings for men to come forward and formally "count" or announce their deeds and often the qualifications for various posts of honor and service were the possession of at least four coups.

The social importance of such deeds naturally developed a kind of heraldry of which the picture writing of the Plains tribes is an example. It was usual to record one's deeds on his buffalo robe, or on the sides of a tipi (Fig. 38). The Dakota had special rules for wearing eagle feathers in the hair, by which one could tell at a glance what deeds the wearer had performed. The Mandan, Assiniboin, and perhaps others, had similar systems. The Dakota carried the idea over into the decorations for horses and clothing. Even the designs upon their moccasins were sometimes made to emblazon the deeds of the wearer.

Chapter III.

RELIGION AND CEREMONIES.

THE sacred beliefs of these Indians are largely formulated and expressed in sayings and narratives having some resemblance to the legends of European peoples. There are available large collections of these tales and myths from the Blackfoot, Crow, Nez Percé, Assiniboin, Gros Ventre, Arapaho, Arikara, Pawnee, Omaha, Northern Shoshoni, and less complete series from the Dakota, Cheyenne, and Ute. In these will be found much curious and interesting information. Each tribe in this area has its own individual beliefs and sacred myths, yet many have much in common, the distribution of the various incidents therein forming one of the important problems in anthropology.

Mythology. A deluge myth is almost universal in the Plains and very widely distributed in the wooded areas as well. Almost everywhere it takes the form of having the submerged earth restored by a more or less human being who sends down a diving bird or animal to obtain a little mud or sand. Of other tales found both within and without the Plains area we may mention, the "Twin-heroes," the "Woman who married a star and bore a Hero," and the "Woman who married a Dog." Working out the distribution of such myths is one of the

fascinating tasks of the folklorist and will some
time give us a clearer insight into the prehistoric
cultural contacts of the several tribes. A typical
study of this kind by Dr. R. H. Lowie will be found
in the Journal of American Folk-Lore, September,
1908, where, for example, the star-born hero is
traced through the Crow, Pawnee, Dakota, Arapaho,
Kiowa, Gros Ventre, and Blackfoot. Indian mythologies often contain large groups of tales each
reciting the adventures of a distinguished mythical
hero. In the Plains, as elsewhere, we find among
these a peculiar character with supernatural attributes, who transforms and in some instances cre-
ates the world, who rights great wrongs, and cor-
rects great evils, yet who often stoops to trivial and
vulgar pranks. Among the Blackfoot, for instance,
he appears under the name of Napiw^a', white old
man, or old man of the dawn. He is distinctly human in form and name. The Gros Ventre, Cheyenne, Arapaho, Hidatsa, and Mandan seem to have
a similar character in their mythology.

The uniqueness of the "White-old-man" appears
when we consider the mythologies of the adjoining
culture areas. Thus between the Plains and the
Pacific Ocean similar tales appear, but are there attributed to an animal character with the name and
attributes of a coyote. Under this name he appears
among the Crow, Nez Percé, and Shoshoni, on the
western fringe of the Plains, but rarely among the
Pawnee, Arikara, and Dakota and practically never

among the tribes designating him as human. Again among the Assiniboin, Dakota, and Omaha, this hero is given a spider-like character (Unktomi). It is thus clear that while the border tribes of the Plains, in common with many other parts of the continent, have an analogous series of tales attributed to animal characters, the tendency at the center is to refer the same tales to a human character. Curiously enough, the names for this character all have in common the ideas of *white* and *east* and were automatically applied to Europeans when first encountered. For these reasons, if no other, the occurrence of a human trickster hero appears as one of the most distinctive characteristics of Plains culture.

Irrespective of the preceding hero cycle, many animal tales are to be found in the Plains. Among these, as in almost every part of the world, we find curious ways of explaining the structural peculiarities of animals as due to some accident; for example, the Blackfoot trickster in a rage tried to pull the lynx asunder whence that animal now has a long body and awkward legs. Such explanations abound in all classes of myths and are considered primary and secondary according to whether they directly explain the present phenomena as in the case of the lynx, or simply narrate an anecdote in which the transformation is a mere incident. Occasionally, one meets with a tale at whose ending the listener is abruptly told that thenceforth things were ordered so and so, the logical connection not being apparent. Probably what happens here is that the native author, knowing it to be customary to explain similar phenomena by mythical occurrences, rather crudely adds the explanation to a current tale. However, not all the animal tales of the Plains function as explanations of origin and transformation, for there are tales in which supernatural beings appear in the form of well-known animals and assist or grant favors to human beings. The buffalo is a favorite character and is seldom encountered in the mythology from other areas. The bear, beaver, elk, eagle, owl, and snake are frequently referred to but also occur in the myths of Woodland and other tribes. Of imaginary creatures the most conspicuous are the water monster and the thunderbird. The former is usually an immense horned serpent who keeps under water and who fears the thunder. The thunderbird is an eagle-like being who causes thunder.

Migration legends and those accounting for the origins and forms of tribal beliefs and institutions make up a large portion of the mythology for the respective tribes and must be carefully considered in formulating a concept of the religion and philosophy of each.

Religious Concepts. To most of us the mention of religion brings to mind notions of God, a supreme overruling and decidedly personal being. Nothing just like this is found among the Indians. Yet, they

seem to have formulated rather complex and abstract notions of a controlling power or series of
powers pervading the universe. Thus, the Dakota
use a term *wakan tanka* which seems to mean, the
greatest sacred ones. The term has often been
rendered as the great mystery but that is not quite
correct. It is true that anything strange and mysterious is pronounced *wakan*, or as having attributes
analogous to *wakan tanka;* but this seems to mean
supernatural. The fact is, as demonstrated by Dr.
J. R. Walker, that the Dakota do recognize a kind of
hierarchy in which the Sun stands first, or as one
of the *wakan tanka*. Of almost equal rank is the
Sky, the Earth, and the Rock. Next in order is another group of four, the Moon (female), Winged-
one, Wind and the "Mediator" (female). Then
come inferior beings, the buffalo, bear, the four
winds and the whirlwind; then come four classes or
groups of beings and so on in almost bewildering
complexity. So far as we know, no other Plains
tribe has worked out quite so complex a conception.
The Omaha *wakonda* is in a way like the Dakota
wakan tanka. The Pawnee recognized a dominating power spoken of as *tirawa*, or "father," under
whom were the heavenly bodies, the winds, the
thunder, lightning, and rain; but they also recognized a sacred quality, or presence, in the phenomena of the world, spoken of as *kawaharu*, a term
whose meaning closely parallels the Dakota *wakan*.
The Blackfoot resolved the phenomena of the uni-

verse into "powers," the greatest and most universal of which is *natosiwa,* or sun power. The sun was in a way a personal god having the moon for his wife and the morningstar for his son. Unfortunately, we lack data for most tribes, this being a point peculiarly difficult to investigate. One thing, however, is suggested. There is tendency here to conceive of some all-pervading force or element in the universe that emanates from an indefinite source to which a special name is given, which in turn becomes an attribute applicable to each and every manifestation of this conceivedly divine element. Probably nowhere, not even among the Dakota, is there a clear-cut formulation of a definite god-like being with definite powers and functions.

A Supernatural Helper. It is much easier, however, to gather reliable data on religious activities or the functioning of these beliefs in actual life. In the Plains, as well as in some other parts of the continent, the ideal is for all males to establish some kind of direct relation with this divine element or power. The idea is that if one follows the proper formula, the power will appear in some human or animal form and will form a compact with the applicant for his good fortune during life. The procedure is usually for a youth to put himself in the hands of a priest, or shaman, who instructs him and requires him to fast and pray alone in some secluded spot until the vision or dream is obtained. In the Plains such an experience results in the conferring of one or more songs, the laying on of certain curious formal taboos, and the designation of some object, as a feather, skin, shell, etc., to be carried and used as a charm or medicine bundle. This procedure has been definitely reported for the Sarsi, Plains-Cree, Blackfoot, Gros Ventre, Crow, Hidatsa, Mandan, Dakota, Assiniboin, Omaha, Arapaho, Cheyenne, Kiowa, and Pawnee. It is probably universal except perhaps among the Ute, Shoshoni, and Nez Percé. We know also that it is frequent among the Woodland Cree, Menomini, and Ojibway. Aside from hunger and thirst, there was no self-torture except among the Dakota and possibly a few others of Siouan stock. With these it was the rule for all desiring to become shamans, or those in close rapport with the divine element, to thrust skewers through the skin and tie themselves up as in the sun dance, to be discussed later.

Now, when a Blackfoot, a Dakota, or an Omaha went out to fast and pray for a revelation, he called upon all the recognized mythical creatures, the heavenly bodies, and all in the earth and in the waters, which is consistent with the conceptions of an illy localized power or element manifest everywhere. No doubt this applies equally to all the aforesaid tribes. If this divine element spoke through a hawk, for example, the applicant would then look upon that bird as the localization or medium for it; and for him, *wakonda,* or what not, was manifest or resided therein; but, of course, not exclusively.

Quite likely, he would keep in a bundle the skin or feathers of a hawk that the divine presence might ever be at hand. This is why the warriors of the Plains carried such charms into battle and looked to them for aid. It is not far wrong to say that all religious ceremonies and practices (all the so-called medicines of the Plains Indians) originate and receive their sanction in dreams or induced visions, all, in short, handed down directly by this wonderful vitalizing element.

Medicine Bundles. In anthropological literature it is the custom to use the term medicine in a technical sense, meaning anything that manifests the divine element. Among the Blackfoot, Arapaho, Crow, Kiowa, Hidatsa, and Mandan especially, and to varying extent among the other tribes of the Plains, the men made extraordinary use of these charms or amulets, which were, after all, little medicine bundles. A man rarely went to war or engaged in any serious undertaking without carrying and appealing to one or more of these small bundles. They usually originated, as just stated, in the dreams or visions of so-called medicinemen who gave them out for fees. With them were often one or more songs and a formula of some kind. Examples of these may be seen in the Museum's Pawnee and Blackfoot collections, where they seem most highly developed.

In addition to these many small individual and more or less personal medicines, many tribes have

more pretentious bundles of sacred objects which
are seldom opened and never used except in connec-

Fig. 39.   Medicine-Pipe Bundle.   Blackfoot.

The Blackfoot Indians formerly maintained a number of sacred
bundles containing pipes and other objects, usually spoken of as
medicine-pipes, the term medicine meaning something animated by
the supernatural (see p. 110).   In all, the Blackfoot possessed seven-
teen of these pipe bundles in 1903.   An elaborate ritual accompanies
each bundle and must be demonstrated whenever the bundle is opened
and the pipe taken out.   The owner of such a bundle is responsible
for its care, the maintenance of its ritual, and the observance of all
the regulations connected therewith.   His position in the tribe is
much the same as that of a priest among us.

The outer wrapping to a pipe bundle is skin of the black bear, the
inner wrappings are of elkskin.   A woman's belt is attached, because on the march the pipe-keeper's wife carries the bundle.   In
the bundle is first of all the great pipe; but there are also skins of
an owl, two loons, two white swans, two cranes, a muskrat, an otter,
a fawn, a prairie dog, a rattle, tobacco, etc.

tion with certain solemn ceremonies.   We refer to
such as the tribal bundles of the Pawnee, the medicine arrows of the Cheyenne, the sacred pipe and

Fig. 40. A Medicine-Pipe. Blackfoot.

This is the great pipe from the bundle shown in the preceding figure. It is believed to have come from the Thunder God and, in
consequence, its presence in a camp gives protection against lightning.
At the sound of the first thunder in the spring of the year, the bundle
is opened, the ritual performed, and the pipe offered to the Thunder
God, as prayers for the welfare of all are uttered by the pipe-keeper.
This type of pipe is found among the Northern Plains tribes while
analogous forms are encountered in other parts of the Plains Area.

the wheel of the Arapaho, the "taimay" image of the Kiowa, the Okipa drums of the Mandan, and the buffalo calf pipe of the Dakota. In addition to these very famous ones, there are numerous similar bundles owned by individuals, especially among the Blackfoot, Sarsi, Gros Ventre, Omaha, Hidatsa, and Pawnee. The best known type of bundle is the medicine-pipe which is highly developed among the Blackfoot and their immediate neighbors. In the early literature of the area frequent reference is made to the calumet or, in this case, a pair of pipe-stems waved in the demonstration of a ritual binding the participants in a firm brotherhood. This ceremony is reported among the Pawnee, Omaha, Ponca, Mandan, and Dakota, and, according to tradition, originated with the Pawnee. The use of either type of pipe bundle seems not to have reached the western tribes. One singular thing is that in all these medicine-pipes it is the stem that is sacred, often it is not even perforated, is frequently without a bowl, and in any event rarely actually smoked. It is thus clear that the whole is highly symbolic.

The war bundles of the Osage have not been investigated but seem to belong to a type widely distributed among the Pawnee, Sauk and Fox, Menomini, and Winnebago of the Woodland area. Among the Blackfoot, there is a special development of the bundle scheme in that they recognize the transferring of bundles and amulets to other persons together with the compact between the original

Fig. 41. A Bundle and Contents. Arapaho.

owner and the divine element. The one receiving the bundle pays a handsome sum to the former owner. This buying and selling of medicines is so frequent that many men have at one time and another owned all the types of bundles in the tribe.

The greatest bundle development, however, seems to rest with the Pawnee, one of the less typical Plains tribes, whose whole tribal organization is expressed in bundle rituals and their relations to each other. For example, the Skidi Pawnee, the tribal division best known, base their religious and governmental authority upon a series of bundles at the head of which is the Eveningstar bundle. The ritual of this bundle recites the order and purpose of the Creation and is called upon to initiate and authorize every important undertaking. The most sacred object in this bundle is an ear of corn, spoken of as 'Mother,' and symbolizing the life of man. Similar ears are found in all the important bundles of the Pawnee and one such ear was carried by a war party for use in the observances of the warpath. From all this we see that the emphasis of Pawnee thought and religious feeling is placed upon cultivated plants in contrast to the more typical Plains tribes who make no attempts at agriculture, but who put the chief stress upon buffalo ceremonies. The tendency to surround the growing of maize with elaborate ceremonies is characteristic of the Pueblo Indians of the Southwest and also of such tribes east of the Mississippi as made a specialty of agriculture.

In the Museum collections are a few important
bundles, a medicine-pipe, and a sun dance bundle
(natoas) from the Blackfoot, the latter a very sacred
thing; an Arapaho bundle; the sacred image used
in the Crow sun dance; an Osage war bundle; a
series of tribal bundles from the Pawnee, etc. To
them the reader is referred for further details.

Tribal Ceremonies. In addition to the above
ceremonial practices, there are a number of pro-
cedures deserving special mention. Most tribes had
a series of ceremonies for calling the buffalo and inducing them to enter the pound or to permit themselves to be easily taken by the hunters. These have
not been satisfactorily investigated but seem to have
varied a great deal probably because this function
was usually delegated to a few tribal shamans each
of whom exercised his own special formulae. The
Crow, the Blackfoot, and perhaps a few other tribes
had elaborate tobacco planting ceremonies. The
Pawnee formerly sacrificed a captured maiden in a
ceremony to the Morningstar, the procedure showing close parallels to Aztec practices, and some of
the maize-growing tribes in this area are credited
with a "green corn" or harvest dance, a characteristic of the tribes east of the Mississippi. The Pawnee also maintained some curious ceremonies in
which shamans performed remarkable tricks and
demonstrated their magical powers. Turning from
these rather exceptional practices, we find certain
highly typical ceremonies.

Fig. 42.   Arapaho Sun Dance, Model in the Museum.

The Sun Dance. One of the most important tribal ceremonies is the so-called sun dance. The name as used in literature is probably derived from the Dakota who speak of one phase of the ceremony as sun-gaze-dancing; i.e., the worshipper gazes steadily at the sun while dancing. To a less extent, this is one of the objective features of the ceremony wherever performed and is occasionally associated with a torture feature in which skewers are thrust through the skin of the breast and back and the devotee suspended or required to dance until the skin gives away, all the time supplicating the sun for divine guidance.

Another feature is that in the center of the ceremonial place is set up a tree, or sun pole, which is scouted for, counted coup upon, and felled, as if it were an enemy. Upon this, offerings of cloth are made to the sun. In the fork at the top is usually a bunch of twigs, in some cases called the nest of the thunderbird. Within the enclosure on the left side an altar is made.

The time of the sun dance is in midsummer. It is usually initiated by the vow of a man or woman to make it as a sacrifice in return for some heeded prayer in time of great danger. The soldier societies, the women's society, and other organizations, generally take turns dancing at the sun pole after the above-named rites have been concluded. As a rule all who perform important functions in the sun dance are required to spend several days in fasting and other purification ceremonies.

Fig. 43. Sun Dance Headdress. Blackfoot.

In so brief an account of the Sun Dance, as permitted in the text, one cannot describe the various types of procedure. While everywhere the Sun Dance is much the same, there are variations in regalia and other details. In Fig. 43 is shown the headdress worn by the woman who initiates the Blackfoot Sun Dance, and which is one of the most sacred objects owned by the tribe. Except at the time of the ceremony, it is kept in a bundle and reverently cared for, as are other medicine bundles.

The sacred bundle of this headdress contains many objects. First of all, is a digging-stick, in some respects more sacred than the headdress itself, because it symbolizes woman's fall and banishment from the skyland, where she dug up the forbidden plant. The other necessary objects, all used in the ritual for the initial Sun Dance ceremony, are, a carrying case of rawhide, a covering of badger skin, bladders for holding feathers, skins of the weasel, squirrel, and gopher. Also, bags of paint, many colors, seven rattlers of buffalo skin, and numerous small objects.

As shown in the drawing, the sacred headdress is built upon a strip of buffalo skin, cut to represent a lizard; one half of it is painted red, the other blue. Hanging down the sides are many strips of white weasel skin. In front, or over the woman's forehead is, first, the entire skin of a white weasel, filled with hair or scalplocks. Under the weasel skin is a crude object, with a ball-like head, spoken of as a doll. For the most part the doll contains tobacco, but attached to its head is a flint arrow-head. A pair of bird skins at the back and plumes for the top complete the headdress.

As in most ceremonial objects of this kind, each is accounted for in the sacred myth on which the ritual is founded. No other Plains tribes have such a headdress, except the Sarsi, but the Crow and Kiowa use a doll-like image in the ceremony.

An exhaustive study of the Sun Dance has been made by the Museum staff and will be found in Volume 16 of the *Anthropological Papers*.

Fig. 43. Sun Dance Headdress. Blackfoot.

Some form of sun dance has been reported for all the tribes of this area except the Comanche, Omaha, Iowa, Kansa, Missouri, Osage, Oto, Pawnee, Wichita, and Nez Percé: that even some of these formerly practised it, is probable. The Mandan had an elaborate ceremony known as the Okipa, fully described by George Catlin who visited that tribe in 1832. This is not a sun dance, but contains the self-torture practised by the Dakota.

When we consider the total distribution of the sun dance it appears that its ceremonial complex, like that for soldier societies (p. 99), presents several features variously combined and distributed. These are the torture, the circular shelter of poles, the use of a sacred bundle, the altar, the erection of a sun pole, and the dancing ceremonies. The form of shelter shown in the Arapaho model has been observed among the Arapaho, Gros Ventre, Kiowa, Ute, Wind River Shoshoni, Cheyenne, Blackfoot, Sarsi, Plains-Cree, and Hidatsa. With the possible exception of the Plains-Cree all used a sacred bundle of some form. (For examples see the Blackfoot and Crow collections.) The Crow used a bundle containing an image, but a different form of shelter. The Ponca and Dakota used no bundles but a shelter of another type from that shown in the model, but both had the torture, sun-gaze-dancing, and the sun pole.

Ghost Dance Ceremonies. Even within historic times, there have been several interesting religious developments among the Plains Indians. The most noted of these was the ghost dance. This was a religious ceremony founded upon the belief in the coming of a Messiah, which seems to have originated among the Paviotso Indians in Nevada (Plateau Area) about 1888 and which spread rapidly among the Indians of the Plains. The prophet of the religion was a young Paiute Indian (Plateau Area) who claimed to have had a revelation while in a delirious condition caused by an attack of fever. The Teton-Dakota seem to have first heard of the new religion in 1889 and in a council held by Red-cloud appointed a committee to visit the prophet and investigate. On this committee were Short-bull and Kicking-bear, who returned very enthusiastic converts and began preaching the new religion among the Dakota. The principal belief was that an Indian Messiah was about to appear to destroy the white race, and restore the buffalo with all former customs. As in all Indian ceremonies, dancing played a large part, but in this case the dancers usually fell into a hypnotic trance and upon recovering recounted their visions and supernatural experiences. All participants were provided with decorated cloth garments bearing symbolic designs which were believed to have such relation with the coming Messiah that all who wore them would be protected from all harm. Among white people these garments were generally known as "bullet proof shirts" (see Dakota collections).

The enthusiasm over the new ghost dance religion spread over the several Dakota Indian reservations, resulting in the attempted arrest and killing of the famous Sitting-bull by the Indian police and hostile demonstrations on the Pine Ridge Reservation, under the leadership of Short-bull and Kicking-bear.

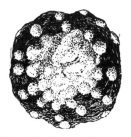

Fig. 44. Peyote Button.

In consequence, United States troops were concentrated on the Pine Ridge Reservation under the command of General Nelson A. Miles. The hostility of the Indians increased until December 29, 1890, when there was an engagement between Big-foot's band and the command of Colonel Forsyth on Wounded Knee Creek, in which thirty-one soldiers and one hundred twenty-eight Indians were killed. In a short time after this decisive engagement, practically all the Indians laid down their arms and abandoned the ghost dance religion. It is probable, however, that some of the ceremonies connected with the ghost dance religion are performed even to this day, since several of the leaders are still living.

Practically all of the typical tribes (p. 19) took up

the new beliefs about the same time but nowhere else did the excitement lead to violence. Among the Cheyenne, Arapaho, and Gros Ventre, the ceremonies still exist in a modified form, apparently combined with the Omaha or grass dance (p. 128).

Peyote Worship. There are curious ceremonies connected with the eating or administering of the dried fruit of a small cactus (*Anhalonium* or *Laphophora*), native of the lower Rio Grande and Mexico. The name "mescal" is wrongly applied to this fruit by many white observers. Long ago, these ceremonies seem to have been known to the Kiowa and Comanche of the Plains and widely distributed in the Southwest and Mexico. The rites begin in the evening and continue until the following dawn, and are restricted to men. There is a definite ritual, a small drum and rattle of special form being essential. Within the last few years, this worship has become general among the Arapaho, Cheyenne, Omaha, Dakota, and Kiowa, and threatens to supplant all other native ceremonies. It is even found among the Winnebago, Sauk and Fox, and Menomini of the Woodlands. This diffusion in historic times makes it one of the most suggestive phenomena for students of Indian life, since it affords an indisputable example of culture diffusion.

Dancing Associations. There are a number of semi-religious festivals or ceremonies in which a large number of individuals participate and which

seem to have been handed on from one tribe to another. The best known example of this is the
Omaha or Grass dance which has been reported for
the Arapaho, Pawnee, Omaha, Dakota, Crow, Gros
Ventre, Assiniboin, and Blackfoot. The various
tribes agree in their belief that this dance and its
regalia originated with the Pawnee. The Dakota
claim to have obtained it directly from the Pawnee
about 1870. The Arapaho and Gros Ventre claim
to have learned it from the Dakota. The Gros
Ventre taught it to the Blackfoot about 1883.
Though these statements of the Indians are not to be
taken as absolutely correct, they indicate that this
dance is a modern innovation. Recently, the Blackfoot have carried the dance to the Flathead and
Kootenai tribes to the west.

The meetings are held at night in large circular
wooden buildings erected for that purpose. Some
of the dancers wear large feather bustles, called
crow belts, and peculiar roached headdresses of hair.
A feast of dog's flesh is served at which many members formally give away property to the poor.
They even go so far, now and then, as to formally
put away a wife as the greatest act of self-denial.

In the same class may be mentioned the kissing
or hugging dance, sometimes called the Cree dance.
This seems to have come from the north and re-
sembles a form of dance once common among the
half-breed Canadians. In the Plains, however, it
has Indian songs and other undoubtedly native

features. To this list may be added the tea dances, the horseback dances, etc.

Among these Indians each distinct ceremony or dance has its own peculiar set of songs to which additions are made from time to time.

War and Scalp Dances. The scalp or some other part of the foe was often carried home and given to the women of the family who made a feast and danced in public with songs and cheers for the victors. A party about to go to war would gather in the evening, sing, dance, and observe certain religious rites to ensure success. In all of these there seems to have been little that was distinctive or peculiar to the Plains.

Ceremonial Procedure. It is rather difficult to characterize satisfactorily the many detailed ceremonies of the Plains, but some points are clear. In most we find an inordinate amount of singing, often extending over an entire day and night, interspersed with prayers and the handling of sacred objects or bundles and occasional dancing. The sweathouse is used for preliminary purification and incense is burned at intervals during the ceremony. The participants usually sit in a circle with a fire at the center. A man leads and has the entire direction of the ritual, other men and perhaps women assisting him. A kind of altar or earth painting is common. This is usually a small square of fresh earth between the leader and the fire upon which symbols are made by dropping dry paint, suggesting the sand painting of the Navajo, but otherwise highly individual in character. In the manipulation of ceremonial objects we often observe four movements or three feints before anything is done. Again, many objects are not put down directly but moved around in a sunwise direction. All such manipulations are likely to be common to all ceremonies and therefore not distinctive or significant.

It is not far wrong to say that all the ceremonies are demonstrations of the ritual associated with some bundle or objects and represent the original visions or experiences in which the whole was handed down. The demonstration seems to be ordered on the theory that, as in the original revelation, the divine element will be present in the objects and appurtenances thereto. The persons participating are rather passive. We have practically no attempts to impersonate and to act out in detail the parts played by supernatural beings. This is shown in the almost entire absence of masks and ceremonial costume. Thus, among the Indians of the North Pacific area, the Pueblos of the Southwest, and the Iroquois of the Woodlands, we find persons in ceremonies dressed and masked to represent the various gods or supernatural creatures and who act out parts of the ritual. Even among the Navajo and the Apache of the Southwest, these costumes play a conspicuous part. All this is rare in the strictly religious ceremonies of the Plains and brings out by contrast what is perhaps one of their most characteristic features.

Painting the face and body and the use of a pipe are also highly developed elements. In most cases, there is a distinct painting for each ceremony, again supposed to be according to the directions of the initial revelation. A lighted pipe is not only frequently passed during a ceremony but is also filled to the accompaniment of ceremonial movements and offered with prayers to many or all of the recognized sources of the higher powers.

The only musical instruments used in these ceremonies are rattles, drums, and whistles.

CHAPTER IV.

DECORATIVE AND RELIGIOUS ART.

THE Plains Indians have a well-developed decorative art in which simple geometric designs are the elements of composition. This art is primarily the work of women. Clothing and other

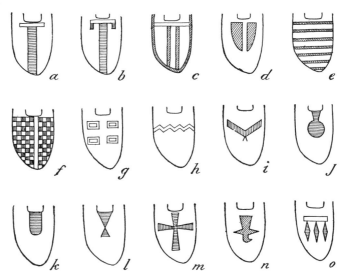

Fig. 45. Types of Designs on Moccasins. (Kroeber.)

useful articles, made of skins, were rendered attractive by designs in beads and quills. Rawhide bags and parfleche (pp. 67–71) were treated with a peculiar type of painting in many colors. Realistic art

132

was practised chiefly by men in the recording of war
deeds (p. 104) and reached a high degree of excel-
lence among the Dakota and Mandan. The technical
aspect of bead and quillwork of the Plains is quite
peculiar. Formerly, there was little or none of the
woven work so common in the Eastern Woodlands
and the forests of Canada, the method here being to
lay the quills on the surface of skins in large geometric areas. The beads now in use were introduced by traders and have almost displaced the
original art of porcupine quill embroidery.

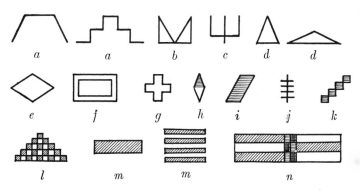

Fig. 46. Design Elements, Bead and Quill Embroidery. (Kroeber.)

The most numerous decorated objects in collections are moccasins which therefore offer an extensive design series. Though often examples of each
design may be found upon the moccasins in a single
tribe, the tendencies are always toward a few tribal
types. Thus, the Arapaho predominate in longi-
tudinal stripes (Fig. 45, a–d), the Dakota in definite

figures (f, g, m, n, o), the Blackfoot in U-shaped figures (k), etc.   Additional designs will be found upon
leggings, bags, and pouches.   All these designs may
be resolved into simple geometrical elements or patterns (Fig. 46).   Here also, tribal preferences are
to be found.   The rawhide paintings are also geometric and though the designs first appear quite
complex, they can readily be resolved into triangles
and rectangles.   Another point of special interest is

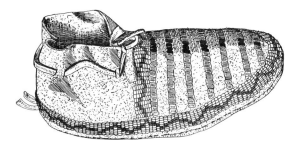

Fig. 47.   Arapaho Moccasin with Symbolic Decoration.

that some tribes give these conventionalized designs
a symbolic value.   This is particularly true of the
Arapaho.

Thus Fig. 47 shows a moccasin which is beaded
around the edges, but has its front surface traversed
by a number of quilled lines.   The white beadwork
represents the ground.   Green zigzag lines upon it
are snakes.   The quilled lines represent sweathouse
poles.   These lines are red, blue, and yellow, and
the colors represent stones of different colors, used
for producing steam in the sweathouse.   At the heel

of the moccasin, which is not shown in the figure, are two small green squares. These represent the blankets with which the sweathouse is covered.

The design of a snake was embroidered on this moccasin in order that the child wearing it might not be bitten by snakes. The symbols referring to the sweathouse were embroidered on the moccasin in order that the child might grow to the age at which the sweathouse is principally used; namely, old age.

The Dakota also have interpretations for their designs but seemingly to a less degree than the Arapaho. Among other tribes, occasional cases of symbolism have been reported. In the Museum collections is a pair of moccasins from the Plains-Ojibway bearing Plains designs and accompanied by a definite symbolic interpretation. All this suggests that there must have one time been a marked undercurrent of symbolism in the art of the Plains.

It was once assumed that when you found in the art of any people a geometric design, said to stand for a definite plant or animal form, the realistic drawing was the original form from which it was derived by a process of conventionalization. When we attempt to apply this principle to the art of the Dakota and the Arapaho, for instance, we find in some cases the same geometrical figure used by both tribes but to symbolize entirely different objects. We are, therefore, forced to assume that there is no necessary connection between the life history of a decorative design and the object it symbolizes. Plains art clearly shows that often along with a style of designs goes also a style or mode of interpretation. Since this interpretation is a reading-in

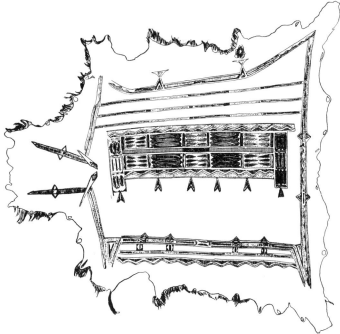

Fig. 48.   Painted Designs on a Woman's Robe.   Dakota.

on the part of those having such a mode, any vague resemblance will suffice.

This is nicely illustrated in the curious U-shaped figure upon the beaded yokes of many woman's dresses. Some Teton-Dakota women once said this had always been known to them as representing a turtle's head and legs as he emerged from the lake (the beaded yoke). Yet, somewhat similar figures occur on the dresses of other tribes from whom no such symbolism has been reported. This might be explained as brought about by the other tribes borrowing the pattern from the Teton; but when many of these garments are examined, we observe that often the U-shaped turn is made to carry the beaded border around the hairy tail of the deer left, or sewed, upon the skin from which the garment was made. The tail tuft naturally falls just below the yoke because the dresses are fashioned by joining the tail ends of two skins by a yoke, or neck piece. Hence, it seems more probable that the pattern was developed as a mere matter of technique and that later on the Teton read into it the symbolism of the turtle, because of some fancied resemblance to that animal and because of some special appropriateness.

The preceding remarks apply exclusively to objects in which the motive was chiefly decorative. There was another kind of art in which the motive was mainly religious, as the paintings upon the Blackfoot tipi, the figures upon the ghost dance shirts of the Dakota, etc. Such drawings, as with heraldry devices (p. 104), were almost exclusively the work of men. Another suggestive point is that this more serious art tends to be realistic in contrast to the highly geometric form of decorative art.

In general, an objective study of this art suggests that the realistic, decorative, and other art seem to

have been greatly developed on the northeastern
border of the area, while the geometric was most
accentuated on the southwestern. Thus on the
northeast, beyond the limit of our area, the Ojibway
especially possessed a highly developed pictographic
type of art while the Ute (Shoshoni) of the extreme
southwest of the area seem to have practised no such
pictographic art but presented in contrast a highly
developed geometric type both in embroidery and
rawhide painting. Taking the Arapaho and Teton-
Dakota as two intermediate groups, we find the
former inclining to the geometric art of their Shoshonean neighbors, while the latter show almost
equal proficiency in the two contrasting types.
Thus, we seem to have two influences from opposite
directions, reinforcing the common suggestion that
the geometric art of this area was introduced from
the southwestern part of the continent.

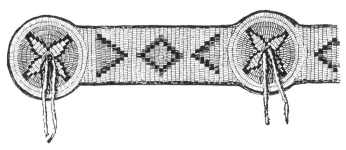

Fig. 49. Blanket Band in Quills. Blackfoot.

Chapter V.

LANGUAGE.

A S STATED at the outset, it is customary to classify peoples according to their languages. The main groups are what are called stock languages, or families. Under such heads are placed all languages that seem to have had a common origin regardless of whether they are mutually intelligible or not. Thus English and German are distinct forms of speech, yet they are considered as belonging to the same stock, or family. In North America, there are more than fifty such families, of which seven have representatives in the Plains. Only one, however, the Kiowa, is entirely confined to the area, though the Siouan and Caddoan are chiefly found within its bounds. The others (Algonkian, Shoshonean, Athapascan, and Shahaptian) have much larger representation elsewhere, which naturally leads us to infer that they must have migrated into the Plains. Though this is quite probable, it cannot be proven from the data at hand, except possibly for the Algonkian-speaking Plains-Ojibway and Cheyenne, of whose recent movement out into the Plains we have historic evidence. These tribes are of special interest to students, since in a comparatively short period of time they put away most of their native culture and took on that of their neighbors in the Plains.

Indians of the Plains, according to Language

Siouan Language

Assiniboin	Mandan
Crow	Missouri
Dakota	Omaha
Hidatsa	Osage
Iowa	Oto
Kansa	Ponca

Algonkian Language

Arapaho	Gros Ventre
Blackfoot	Plains-Cree
Cheyenne	Plains-Ojibway

Caddoan Language

Arikara Pawnee

Wichita

Kiowan Language

Kiowa

Shoshonean Language

Bannock	Northern Shoshoni
Comanche	Ute

Wind River Shoshoni

Athapascan Language

Kiowa-Apache Sarsi

Shahaptian Language

Nez Percé

The Athapascan-speaking Kiowa-Apache and Sarsi are also worthy of notice because the family to which they belong has representatives in five of the eight great culture areas into which North American cultures are localized, affording us the unique example of five distinct cultures with languages of the same family, or stock.

Returning to our classification of Plains tribes under linguistic families, it may be well to note that while it is absolutely true that these families have nothing in common, the differences between the various tribes under the same stock are by no means equal. Thus, while a Dakota and an Assiniboin can make themselves partially understood, Dakota and Crow are so different that only philologists are able to discover them to be of the same family. Again, in the Algonkian group, the Arapaho and Gros Ventre are conscious of having related languages, while the Blackfoot lived on neighborly terms with the latter for many years as did the Cheyenne with the Arapaho, not once, so far as we know, discovering any definite relation between their languages. It is well to remember, therefore, that the term linguistic stock does not denote the language or speech of a particular tribe, but is a designation of the philologists to define observed relationships in structure and form, and that the speech of these Indians differs in varying degree as one passes from one group to the other. Thus, the seven tribes of the Dakota form at least three dialectic groups:

the Eastern tribes say Dakota and the Teton, La-
kota, one always using *d* for the other's *l;* the Santee *hda* (go home), the Teton *gla,* and the Yankton
kda. Even within the different communities of the
Teton small differences are said to exist. Hence,
the differences in speech are after all gradations of
variable magnitude from the study of which philologists are able to discover relationship and descent,
all believed to have originated from one now extinct
mother tongue, being classed under one family, or
stock name. In short, there are no language characters peculiar to the Plains tribes, as is the case
with other cultural characters.

The foregoing remarks apply entirely to oral language. We must not overlook the extensive use of
a sign language which seems to have served all the
purposes of an international or intertribal language.
The signs were made with the hands and fingers, but
were not in any sense the spelling out of a spoken
language. The language was based upon ideas
alone. Had it been otherwise, it could not have
been understood outside of the tribe. Though some
traces of such a language have been met with outside of the Plains, it is only within the area that we
find a system so well developed that intertribal
visitors could be entertained with sign-talk on all
subjects. The Crow, Kiowa, Arapaho, Cheyenne,
and Blackfoot are generally regarded as having
been most proficient and the Omaha, Osage, Kansas
and Ute, as least skilful in its use. It may not be

amiss to add that in most tribes could be found individuals priding themselves in speaking one or more languages. In former times, many Nez Percé, Blackfoot, Gros Ventre, Dakota, and Mandan are said to have known some of the Crow language which was in consequence often used by traders. This, if true, was no doubt due to the peculiar geographical position of the Crow. The sign language, however, could be used among all tribes familiar with it and must, therefore, be considered one of the striking peculiar traits of the Plains and an important factor in the diffusion of culture.

Chapter VI.

PHYSICAL TYPE.

S O FAR we have concerned ourselves with how the Plains Indians lived, or with their culture, but our subject would not be complete without a general idea of their anatomy and physical condition. According to the census of 1910 there resided within the United States 50,208 members of the tribes we have designated as Plains Indians. The number for each tribe, together with the extent of mixture, is shown in the table. Nearly all of the mixed-bloods are descendants of white men and Indian women. We have no exact data as to the number of these Indians in Canada, but consider it to be less than 12,000. Since 1880 there seems to have been little change in the density of this population, though some tribes are now increasing. As to how the number of 1910 compares with the population of a century or more ago we can but guess, but there is no reason to believe that it ever exceeded 100,000.

No careful study of the physical types for the Plains has been made. Our general impression of the tribal appearance is largely influenced by hair dress, costume, and posture, and it is difficult to dissociate these externals from somatic features. Yet,

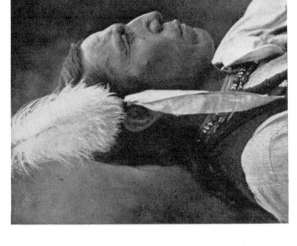

TETON-DAKOTA.

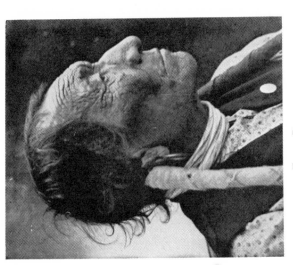

CROW.

145

PAWNEE.

CHEYENNE.

146

Wind River Shoshoni.
(Bureau Ethnology Photo.)

147

Blackfoot.
(Blood Tribe.)

148 INDIANS OF THE PLAINS

a brief scrutiny of casts of faces or photographs
usually reveals tribal resemblances like those we see
in families among ourselves. As the Indians of the
Plains are but a subdivision of the same race, this is

POPULATION AND MIXTURE OF BLOOD.

Tribe.	Total Population.	Percentage Full-Bloods.	Tribe.	Total Population.	Percentage Full-Bloods.
Teton-Dakota	14284	74.2	Omaha	1105	80.1
Shoshoni	3840	86.7	Sioux (miscellane-		
Cheyenne	3055	87.1	ous)	996	49.6
Sisseton Dakota	2514	64.9	Ponca	875	52.7
Piegan	2268	53.5	Pawnee	633	85.9
Ute	2240	94.1	Hidatsa	547	76.4
Yankton Dakota	2088	64.6	Iowa	547	24.2
Crow	1799	69.0	Gros Ventre	510	76.5
Eastern Dakota	1539	51.9	Caddo	452	74.3
Arapaho	1419	92.4	Arikara	444	83.8
Osage	1373	43.0	Bannock	413	78.2
Yanktonai Dakota	1357	84.3	Oto	332	63.6
Nez Percé	1259	77.0	Wichita	318	96.9
Assiniboin	1253	63.3	Kansa	238	29.8
Comanche	1171	62.9	Mandan	209	78.9
Kiowa	1126	72.6			
Average percentage of full-bloods		70.00	Total population		50208
			Total full-blood population		35000

about the only difference that should be expected.
The color tone of the skin (a reddish chocolate)
seems about the same throughout the area, though
perhaps lighter with occasional leanings toward the
yellow among some Blackfoot of the north; yet to
be exact, no color studies worthy of the name have
been made. The hair is, like that of all Indians,
uniformly black and straight. As to stature, they
appear rather tall. The following average meas-
urements have been reported.

	Millimeters.	Inches.
Cheyenne	1745	68.7
Crow	1732	68.1
Arapaho	1728	68.03
Dakota	1726	67.09
Plains-Ojibway	1723	67.8
Blackfoot	1715	67.5
Kiowa	1709	67.2
Comanche	1678	66.06

These are from the typical nomadic group of tribes as previously defined and with the exception of the Comanche are quite tall. As the figures above are averages, we must expect among the Cheyenne some very tall individuals. (Twenty percent of those measured, exceeded 1820 mm.)

On the west, the statures are less:

	Millimeters.	Inches.
Nez Percé	1697	66.8
Ute	1661	65.4

Among the village group we note:

	Millimeters.	Inches.
Omaha	1732	68.1
Pawnee	1713	67.4
Arikara	1690	66.5

again a tendency toward tall statures.

So, as compared not only with other Indians, but with mankind as a whole, the Indians of the Plains are a tall people.

Looking at the faces of the various tribes, some general differences appear. Those of the Blackfoot, Plains-Cree, and Assiniboin seem rather rounded and delicate while those of the Dakota are longer and clear cut with strong lines, an eagle nose, and more prominent cheek bones. The Pawnee again have large, heavy, or massive faces. On none of these points, however, have investigations been made and it is an open question whether anything would be accomplished thereby other than the definition of minute differences. In historical times, at least, there was a great deal of intermarriage and visiting between these tribes, which must have tended to level down somatic differences and which makes the successful determination of genetic relationship quite improbable. As to head form, we find an index of about 80 for the Ute, Cree, Dakota, Blackfoot, Cheyenne, Arapaho, Pawnee, and a considerably higher value for the Comanche, Osage, Omaha, Wichita, and Kiowa.

Thus in general it appears that the Indians of the Plains are not anatomically distinct from those occupying some other parts of the continent. Yet, when closely considered they tend to form a group in distinction to the tribes of other areas. In the preceding chapters we observed that the tribes in the center of the Plains were more original in culture, whereas those on the borders had assimilated many foreign traits. So in much the same way we find that the central tribes tend to be tall, while the marginal ones are shorter, like those of the neighboring culture areas. The same kind of differences appear in other characters. It is thus plain that the Indians of the Plains are somewhat distinct from other Indians, but these differences are small as compared with the differences between Indians and Europeans.

CHAPTER VII.

THE CHRONOLOGY OF PLAINS CULTURE.

SO FAR we have sought to sketch the outline for a mental picture of what Plains Indian life was like a half century ago. We have given no consideration to what it was before the discovery of the New World, how these people worked out their food problems, whence they came, the ideas that led to their most characteristic inventions; in short, the course of their culture history. The data for a history of any culture come from three sources, direct observation of the living people, written records, and archaeological remains. So far we have depended almost entirely upon observations made upon the living, that is, we have carefully sifted and compiled the facts reported by contemporary writers. Since the Plains Indians had no native system of writing there are no records of the past and so nothing is to be expected from that source. Thus the only additional aid we may expect would come from archaeology, or the study of objects and traces of culture preserved in the ground. This limitation to the information available for a history of Plains culture divides our subject into two periods: the historic period and the prehistoric. These terms are, however, not the best because the historic period for the Plains Indians opens about 1540, while we think of history as beginning a few thousand years before Christ. It is therefore less confusing to speak of the prehistoric period of the American Indians as pre-Columbian. So from the information at hand we can make the accompanying outline of Plains history or, as we frequently say, the chronology of its culture. To make it easier to understand this chapter, we should fix in our minds the following characteristics of Plains culture:

They lived in the open grass land of the Great West.

The buffalo is the keynote to their culture.

About 1540 they became horse Indians, but before that date used the dog for a beast of burden.

The most typical tribes made no pottery, nor attempted agriculture, but lived in tipis and roamed the open plains.

Chronology of Plains Culture.

1880–——   Reservation Period.

Gradual Americanization and disappearance of native culture traits.

Extinction of the buffalo.

Many objects illustrated in this book and exhibited in the Museum were made in the early part of this period, but are typical of the preceding.

1540–1880   Horse Culture Period.

The culture described in this book belongs here, but many customs, objects, and decorative designs observed in this period seem to have originated in the pre-Columbian.

Probable intensification of roving habits, buffalo hunting, and the use of skins.

Firearms and other trade objects introduced.

Trade beads substituted for quills.

Horses, saddles, and the art of riding introduced.

——–1540   Pre-Columbian Period.

Quillwork introduced.

Agriculture, pottery, and simple weaving appear among the border tribes, but buffalo hunting the chief occupation.

Dog traction developed.

Beginning of buffalo culture, probably very ancient.

The first immigrants brought the use of stone and bone tools.

The Pre-Columbian Period. Though the lands of the New World were first sighted in 1492 it is not until 1540 that we hear of the Plains Indians. At about this time two famous Spanish expeditions

reached the southern corners of the area.   De Soto
came to the Mississippi in 1541 and made some excursions into the prairies to the west.   A year
earlier Coronado set out from a camp near what is
now New Mexico, and traversed the plains north-
eastward, apparently to the country of the Pawnee.
It is from the reports of these two romantic journeys
that we get our first glimpse of Plains culture.
Coronado, at least, saw typical roving Plains Indians, for we read:

. . . They have better figures, are better warriors, and are more
feared.   They travel like the Arabs, with their tents and troops of
dogs loaded with poles and having Moorish pack saddles with girths.
When the load gets disarranged, the dogs howl, calling some one to
fix them right.   These people eat raw flesh and drink blood.   They
do not eat human flesh.   They are a kind people and not cruel.   They
are faithful friends.   They are able to make themselves very well
understood by means of signs.   They dry the flesh in the sun, cutting
it thin like a leaf, and when dry they grind it like meal to keep it
and make a sort of sea soup of it to eat.   A handful thrown into a
pot swells up so as to increase very much.   They season it with fat,
which they always try to secure when they kill a cow.   They empty
a large gut and fill it with blood, and carry this around the neck to
drink when they are thirsty.   When they open the belly of a cow,
they squeeze out the chewed grass and drink the juice that remains
behind, because they say that this contains the essence of the stomach.
They cut the hide open at the back and pull it off at the joints, using
a flint as large as a finger, tied in a little stick, with as much ease
as if working with a good iron tool.   They give it an edge with their
own teeth.   The quickness with which they do this is something worth
seeing and noting.   (Winship, Coronado, 111–112.)
. . . They do not live in houses, but have some sets of poles which
they carry with them to make some huts at the places where they
stop, which serve them for houses.   They tie these poles together at
the top and stick the bottoms into the ground, covering them with
some cowskins which they carry around, and which, as I have said,
serve them for houses.   From what was learned of these Indians, all

their human needs are supplied by these cows, for they are fed and
clothed and shod from these.   They are a people who wander around
here and there, wherever seems to them best.   (Winship, Coronado,
.230.)

It was more than a hundred years later that the
French and English first came in contact with the
northern part of the Plains area, and made similar
observations which may be consulted in the books
treating of Hennepin, Radisson, Perrot, and La
Salle.   From all these accounts we learn that Plains
culture in 1600 was very much like what could have
been observed in 1800, if we ignore horses, guns,
and all other trade articles.   Hence, we can safely
say that the greater part of the culture traits described in the preceding pages originated in pre-
Columbian times.   Our next problem, then, is to determine which of these originated first.

To assign relative ages to pre-Columbian advances
in Plains culture we can proceed only by interpret-
ing the facts at hand.   A people living in tents and
packing their belongings with a few dogs could
scarcely be expected to leave behind them ruins or
earthworks, but only traces of camp fires, heaps of
bones, and here and there a stone tool.   This is just
what the archaeologists have been able to find in the
area occupied by the typical tribes, named and lo-
cated in our introductory chapter.   Of stone objects, there are arrow-heads, lance heads, knives,
scraper blades, grooved hammers, and club heads,
grooved rubbing stones for smoothing arrowshafts,

pipes, etc. Bone objects are not so indestructible
as the preceding, but when surviving consist of skin-
dressing tools, awls and other perforators, wedges,
pattern markers on skins, quill flatteners, knives,
arrow points, whistles, beads, and other ornaments.
Pottery is absent. Thus even a general enumera-
tion of the objects found in archaeological collections from the heart of the Plains indicates that the
tribes of the buffalo country never rose above the
cultural level of nomadic hunters.

Though it is true that no ruins or earthworks are
to be found out in the Plains there are some evi-
dences of habitation. Camping places are marked
by circles of stones used to hold down the edges of
tipis, the lines of old buffalo and antelope drives are
marked by boulders, and occasionally there are
heaps of stones. But of far greater impressiveness
are the great "diggings" from which came the stone
for knives and arrow-heads. The most extensive of
these is known as the "Spanish Diggings" in Con-
verse County, Wyoming, but many others of about
equal magnitude are found in that part of the State.
Each of these covers many acres, one pit after another from which were dug blocks of quartzite and
jasper, and around them heaps of broken blocks,
chips, and rejected forms. Tons and tons of this
worked-over material lie heaped about as evidence
of the antiquity and reality of pre-Columbian Plains
culture. Hence in this earlier period as well as in
later historic time, the Plains were occupied by
stone age hunters.

Unfortunately all of these interesting traces of the pre-Columbian Plains Indians have not been studied closely enough to tell us much about their age, but by comparing the facts of Plains culture with those of the surrounding parts of the continent and especially by studying the cultures of the border Plains tribes some conclusions as to the relative ages for a few culture traits have been formed. These are presented in the chronological table.

The Horse Culture Period. The Indians of the Plains lived a free life until long after the Civil War. The European invasion of the New World brought him the horse, an animal far superior to his dog. Just when and how the horse came into his hands we do not know, but most of the typical tribes seem to have been mounted long before 1700. Both De Soto and Coronado brought many horses into the Plains, some of which escaped, starting wild herds, and the Spanish settlements in New Mexico gave the Indian ample opportunity to learn their use. Once the Indians of the extreme south came to use horses, their spread northward from tribe to tribe would not be long delayed. At least all the tribes west of the Missouri had horses when the French and English explorers first met them.

It is worth noting that most of these tribes became horsemen before they saw Europeans, or were otherwise influenced by traders. Thus Plains horse culture, though introduced by Europeans, was self supporting. The Indian made his own saddles, etc., while his herds increased by natural laws. Had connection with the Old World been broken, it is safe to assume that horse culture would have flourished indefinitely. This is in contrast to the other European traits introduced to the Plains after 1700. The Indian never learned to make guns, powder, cloth, kettles, knives, etc.; hence, these never became a part of his culture in the same sense as the horse. For this reason we characterize the historic period in the development of the Plains Indians as the period of horse culture.

During the long interval from 1540 to 1850, or thereabout, these horse-using Indians roamed the plains at will except as intertribal hostilities and occasional white intrusion prevented, but from 1850 to 1880 settlers began to crowd into the territory, occupy the lands, and exterminate the buffalo. Then followed a period of Indian wars, the establishment of reservations and the gradual subjection of all tribes to white control and close confinement to their reserved lands. By 1880 these methods had completely exterminated the buffalo and all but brought the typical culture of the Plains Indian to an end. Now he sends his children to school, supports churches, cultivates the land, and acquires citizenship.

The establishment of reservations for the Plains Indians began about 1855, but it was not until 1880 or later that all were settled and confined to definite tracts. The first Europeans to visit America treated the Indians as independent nations and their chiefs as the equals of kings. The same attitude was taken by the United States under President Washington so that the chief of each little tribe was recognized as a ruler and treaties were made with him by all succeeding Presidents until the time of Grant, when, in 1871, Congress declared all Indians subjects of the United States. This was the first important step to the assimilation of the Indian, a process which has now progressed so far that all Plains Indians will soon be citizens and their reservations disappear. This not far distant event will mark the close of the last period in the history of Plains culture. Yet the memory of this culture during the horse period will long remain as a source of inspiration for art and literature. No other culture is so picturesque as this, and certainly none holds a higher place in modern art.

CHAPTER VIII.

ORIGINS.

THIS brief sketch of the anthropology of the Plains naturally raises a few quite fundamental questions: How did these tribes come to be here? How long have they been here? What was the origin of their cultures? While final answers cannot be given for these, some progress toward their solution has been made. Taking the cultural classification as our point of view, we see that Plains Indians are not peculiar in stature or head form, yet seem to fall into a group distinct from other parts of the continent. These differences are, however, slight and give us no insight into the origins of the tribal groups. For example, the shorter western tribes ranging from 165 to 170 cm. fall into a large group of low statures including most of the Californian, Plateau, North Pacific Coast, and Southeastern areas. The Comanche, who speak a language of Shoshonean stock widely distributed over the Plateau area, are also relatively short. The greater part of the typical and Village tribes, however, range from 170 to 175 cm., including the Yuma, Mohave, and Pima of the Southwest, the Iroquois and most Algonkin of the Woodland area. As to head form, the moderately long head of the Plains does not hold for the Osage and Wichita of

161

the south and the Nez Percé of the northwest, but extends over the Plateau area on the west and into the Woodland area of the east. Hence, in a general way, the tall, somewhat long-headed, typical tribes seem to have relatives to the east in the Woodlands through Indiana, Ohio, and New York. Possibly this represents the influence of some older parent group whose blood gradually worked its way across the continent through many languages and several varieties of culture. On the other hand, the shorter, less long-headed tribes were massed around the Plains in the Southwest, the Plateaus, and part of the Woodlands, almost engulfing the taller group. Now, while it seems clear that migrations of blood are in evidence, there is, as yet, no satisfactory means of determining the point of origin and the direction of movement for these types. Turning from physical type to language, we have several large masses impinging upon the Plains and while it seems most likely that the parent speech for each stock arose somewhere outside the Plains, we are not yet clear as to the impossibility of their arising in the Plains and spreading to other cultures. It does not seem probable that all of them would arise within this small area, but, on the other hand, it is impossible to give satisfactory proof for any particular tribe. Thus, language gives us but a presumption in favor of migrations into the Plains of the Siouan, Caddoan, and Shoshonean speaking tribes. It is true that many tribes have migration legends some of which are consistent with a few details of culture; but as these nearly always take the forms of other myths, they cannot be given much historical weight. The plain fact is that the moment we get beyond the period of exploration in the Plains, historical data fail us. We know where the tribes were when discovered and most of their movements since that date, but beyond that we must proceed by inference and the interpretation of anthropological data.

Not being able to discover how the various tribes came to be in the Plains, we can scarcely expect to tell how long they have been there. The archaeological method may be brought into play here; but as yet we lack sufficient data. Mounds and earthworks have been discovered in the Dakotas and southward along the Missouri, apparently the fringe of the great mound area in the Woodlands to the east, but in the open plains we have so far only evidence of states of culture similar to those we have just described, from which we infer that no other culture preceded this one. Yet for all we know, its origin may date back several thousand years. Certain it is that in 1540 all the typical Plains traits of culture were in function, and since the wheels of primitive progress move slowly we can safely assume a remote origin.

Anyway when we consider the culture of the Plains since 1540, it appears that so many of the traits enumerated in these pages are almost entirely peculiar to the area that we are constrained to conclude that they developed within it. This is strengthened by the peculiar adaptation of many of these traits to the geographical conditions, suggesting that they were invented or discovered by a Plains people. It seems, therefore, that while the origin of the blood and languages of the Plains cannot be determined, its cultural problem is in a fair way to be solved. Among the most distinctive traits are the sun dance, a camp circle band system, the soldier societies, highly developed ritualistic bundles, a peculiar geometric decorative art, the use of the horse and travois, the skin-covered tipi, the earth-lodge, and economic dependence upon the buffalo. Some of these are absolutely confined to the area and though others are found elsewhere they occur as secondary rather than as primary traits. We may safely conclude, therefore, that the tribes of the Plains at least developed these traits to their present form, if they did not actually invent them. Miss Semple favors the theory that a Plains region is the most favorable environment for the diffusion of cultural traits. Whatever may be the fate of this hypothesis, it is clear that among the Indians of the Plains there has been sufficient diffusion to carry many traits over the greater part of the area. That diffusion rather than independent development or convergent evolution is the most satisfactory explanation of this case, may be seen from noting that the various tribes were acquainted with many of their neighbors, that in the sign language they had a ready means of intercommunication, and that since their discovery the actual diffusion of several traits has been observed by anthropologists.

Perhaps the most interesting phase of Plains anthropology is the general diffusion of traits among the many political and linguistic units found therein.

BIBLIOGRAPHY.

The following is not offered as a complete bibliography of the subject but as a list of books likely to meet the needs of the general reader. For a mere view of Indian life on the Plains, the books of Catlin, Grinnell, Maximilian, and McClintock are recommended.

Annual Reports, Bureau of American Ethnology, 3d, 11th, 13th, 14th, 17th, 22d, 27th.

Anthropological Papers, American Museum of Natural History, Vols. 1, 2, 4, 5, 7, 9, 11, 15, 16, 17, 21, and 25.

Anthropological Series, Field Museum of Natural History, Vols. 4 and 9.

Bulletin, American Museum of Natural History, Vol. 18.

Catlin, George. Illustrations of the Manners, Customs, and Conditions of the North American Indians. London, 1848.

Clark, W. P. The Indian Sign Language. Philadelphia, 1885.

Dodge, Richard I. Our Wild Indians. Hartford, 1882.

Farrand, Livingston. Basis of American History, 1500–1900. The American Nation: a History, Vol. 2. New York, 1904.

Grinnell, George Bird. Blackfoot Lodge Tales. New York, 1904.
Pawnee Hero Stories and Folk-Tales. New York, 1893.
The Story of the Indian. New York, 1904.
The Fighting Cheyennes. New York, 1915.
The Cheyenne Indians, Their History and Ways of Life. 2 vols. New Haven, 1923.

Handbook of American Indians. Washington, 1907, 1910.

Henry and Thompson. New Light on the Early History of the Great Northwest. Edited by Elliott Coues. New York, 1897.

Lewis and Clark. Original Journals of the Lewis and Clark Expedition. (Thwaites Edition.) New York, 1904.

167

Lewis and Clark. History of the Expedition under the Command of Captains Lewis and Clark to the Sources of the Missouri, across the Rocky Mountains, down the Columbia River to the Pacific in 1804–6. Three volumes. New York, 1902.

Mason, Otis T. The Origins of Inventions: A Study of Industry among Primitive Peoples. London, 1895.

Maximilian, Prince of Wied. Travels in the Interior of North America. Translated by H. Evans Lloyd. London, 1843.

McClintock, Walter. The Old North Trail. London, 1910.

McLaughlin, James. My Friend the Indian. Boston and New York, 1900.

Mooney, James. The Cheyenne Indians. (Memoirs, American Anthropological Association, Vol. 1, Part 6, pp. 357–642. Lancaster, Pa., 1907.)

Paget, Amelia M. The People of the Plains. Toronto, 1909.

Papers of the Peabody Museum, Harvard University. Vol. 3, No. 4.

Perrot, Nicolas. The Indian Tribes of the Upper Mississippi Valley and Region of the Great Lakes. Translated, edited, annotated and with bibliography and index by Emma Helen Blair. Two volumes. Cleveland, 1911.

Wilson, Gilbert L. Waheenee, an Indian Girl's Story. St. Paul, Minnesota, 1921.

Winship, George Parker. Editor. The Journey of Coronado, 1540–1542, from the City of Mexico to the Grand Cañon of the Colorado and the Buffalo Plains of Texas, Kansas, and Nebraska, as told by himself and his followers. Translated and edited, with an introduction, by George Parker Winship. New York, 1904.

Wissler, Clark. The American Indian. An Introduction to the Anthropology of the New World. New York, 1917, 1922.

INDEX.